Skeleton

Our body's framework

Contributors

Author: **Jinny Johnson BA FZSL** is a writer and editor of books for children and adults on natural history and science. She is also the author of *Breathing: How we use air* in this series.

Series consultant: **Richard Walker BSc PhD PGCE** taught biology, science and health education for several years before becoming a full-time writer. He is a foremost author and consultant specializing in books for adults and children on human biology, health and natural history. He is the author of *Heart: How the blood gets around the body*, *Making Life: How we reproduce and grow*, *Muscles: How we move and exercise* and *Brain: Our body's nerve centre* in this series.

Advisory panel

1 Heart: How the blood gets around the body
P M Schofield MD FRCP FICA FACC FESC is Consultant Cardiologist at Papworth Hospital, Cambridge

2 Skeleton: Our body's framework
R N Villar MS FRCS is Consultant Orthopaedic Surgeon at Cambridge BUPA Lea Hospital and Addenbrooke's Hospital, Cambridge

3 Digesting: How we fuel the body
J O Hunter FRCP is Director of the Gastroenterology Research Unit, Addenbrooke's Hospital, Cambridge

4 Making Life: How we reproduce and grow
Jane MacDougall MD MRCOG is Consultant Obstetrician and Gynaecologist at the Rosie Maternity Hospital, Addenbrooke's NHS Trust, Cambridge

5 Breathing: How we use air
Mark Slade MA MBBS MRCP is Senior Registrar, Department of Respiratory Medicine, Addenbrooke's Hospital, Cambridge

6 Senses: How we connect with the world
Peter Garrard MA MRCP is Medical Research Council Fellow and Honorary Specialist Registrar, Neurology Department, Addenbrooke's Hospital, Cambridge

7 Muscles: How we move and exercise
Jumbo Jenner MD FRCP is Consultant, and **R T Kavanagh MD MRCP** is Senior Registrar, Department of Rheumatology, Addenbrooke's Hospital, Cambridge

8 Brain: Our body's nerve centre
Peter Garrard MA MRCP is Medical Research Council Fellow and Honorary Specialist Registrar, Neurology Department, Addenbrooke's Hospital, Cambridge

UNDER THE MICROSCOPE

Skeleton

Our body's framework

Jinny Johnson

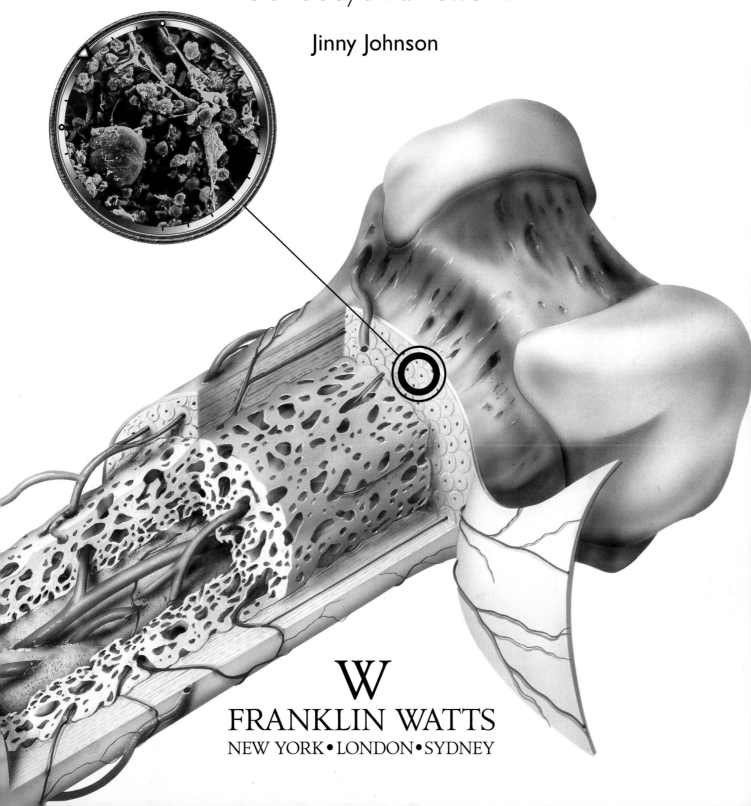

W

FRANKLIN WATTS

NEW YORK • LONDON • SYDNEY

ABOUT THIS BOOK

First published in 1998

Franklin Watts
96 Leonard Street
London EC2A 4RH

Franklin Watts Australia
14 Mars Road
Lane Cove
NSW 2066

© Franklin Watts 1998

0 7496 3071 X

Dewey Decimal Classification Number: 611

A CIP catalogue record for this book is available from the British Library

Printed in Belgium

Produced for Franklin Watts
by Miles Kelly Publishing
Unit 11
The Bardfield Centre
Great Bardfield
Essex
CM7 4SL

Designed by Full Steam Ahead

Illustrated by Mike Saunders

Artwork commissioned by
Branka Surla

Picture research by Yannick Yago

Under the Microscope uses micro-photography to allow you to see right inside the human body.

The camera acts as a microscope, looking at unseen parts of the body and zooming in on the body's cells at work. Some of the micro-photographs are magnified hundreds of times, others thousands of times. They have been dramatically coloured to bring details into crisp focus, and are linked to clear and accurate illustrations that fit them in context inside the body.

New words are explained the first time that they are used, and can also be checked in the glossary at the back of the book.

Bones in close-up
Below, diagrams explain how a baby's soft cartilage skeleton gradually hardens and turns to bone. A photograph of the inside of a bone (left), taken by a powerful microscope (top), zooms in to show a detail of this hardening process in action.

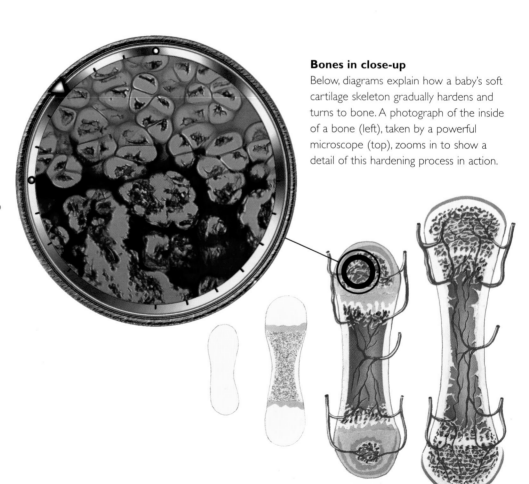

CONTENTS

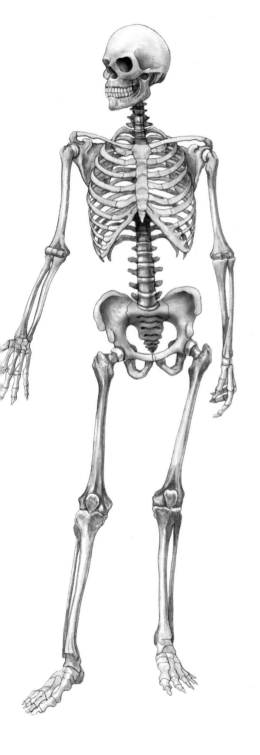

INTRODUCTION

The skeleton is often seen as a symbol of death. Bony forms dance on Halloween costumes and pirate flags bear a skull and crossbones. Skeletons are thought of as something to be frightened of, to keep away from on dark nights. But without your skeleton, you could not live. It is the skeleton that keeps your body in shape, protects your vital organs, such as the heart, brain and lungs, and enables you to move.

The skeleton is an amazing piece of engineering. Enormously strong, it is still very light. A skeleton made of steel of equal strength would weigh at least five times as much. The bones that make up the skeleton are living parts of the body. They are constantly growing and renewing themselves, and blood cells are made in the jellylike marrow inside bones. Bones can stand hard knocks and even repair themselves if broken. It is easy to feel your body's bones. Tap your head and you feel your skull. Bend your fingers and you see the separate finger bones.

But science now enables us to examine our bones in detail through X-rays and scans. These allow doctors to see what has gone wrong if we do suffer from injuries to bones or any bone disease. This volume of **Under the Microscope** zooms in on the body's framework and looks at the amazing skeleton – what bones are made of and how they grow, how the skeleton fits together and how joints move.

The amazing hand
Each hand contains an astonishing 27 bones, making a complex structure that allows us to perform a wide range of movements.

The skull
The bones of the skull give the face its structure and each of us our individual appearance. This image of the structure of the skull has been produced by taking a number of X-rays through the head and combining them on a computer.

Replacing a damaged hip
A new head of stainless steel has been fitted to the top of the femur and a plastic cup placed in the hip bone (left).

The marrow factory
Blood cells for the whole body are produced in the red marrow at the centre of bones (right).

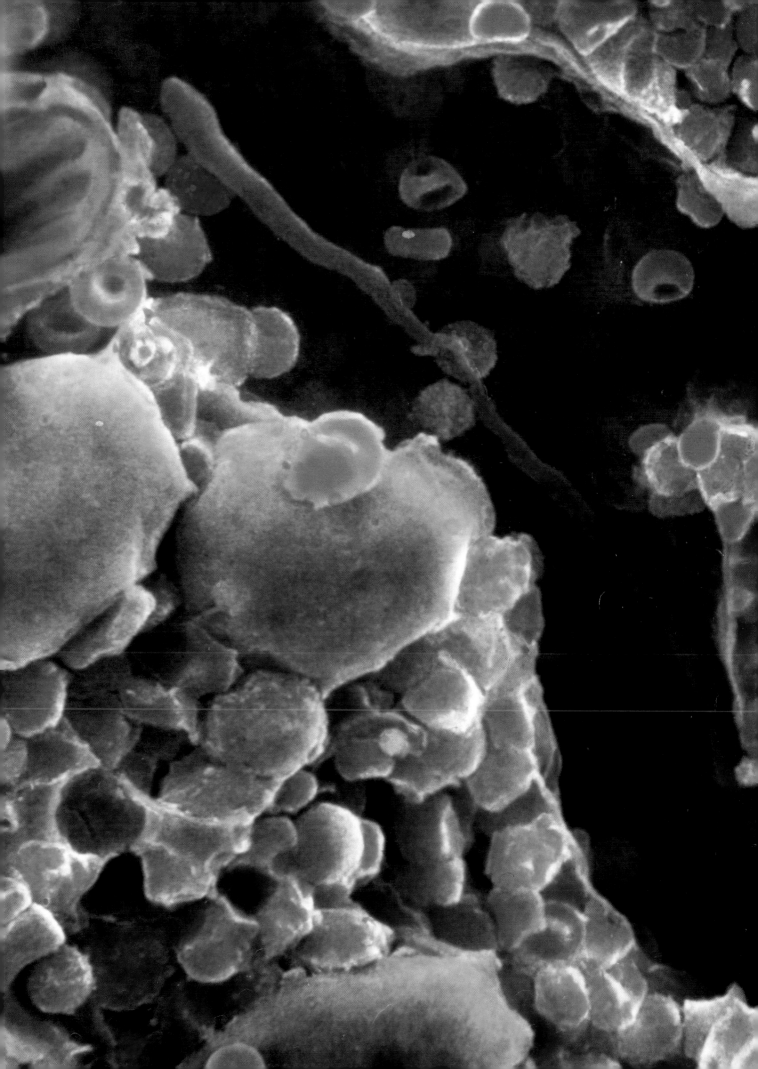

THE BODY'S FRAMEWORK

Bones are the body's support. Without a skeleton, your body would be like a jelly and fall into a shapeless mass on the floor.

Most adults have about 206 bones – some people have extra ribs, some fewer than normal. But, surprisingly, when you are born you have more bones – about 350. Some of these bones join together as you grow. The skeleton is also important because it protects delicate parts inside the body. The skull saves the brain from getting knocked or damaged; the ribs and breastbone protect the heart and lungs. The skeleton's third function is to help the body move. Bones provide a base for muscles, and the long leg and arm bones are levers for movement.

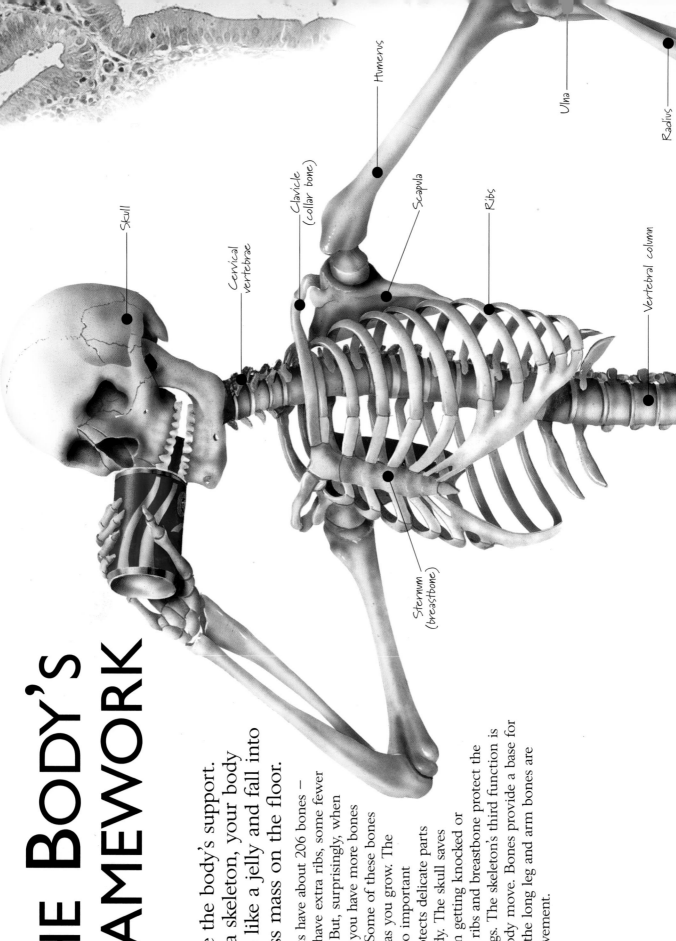

Skull

Cervical vertebrae

Clavicle (collar bone)

Humerus

Ulna

Radius

Scapula

Ribs

Vertebral column

Pelvis

Sternum (breastbone)

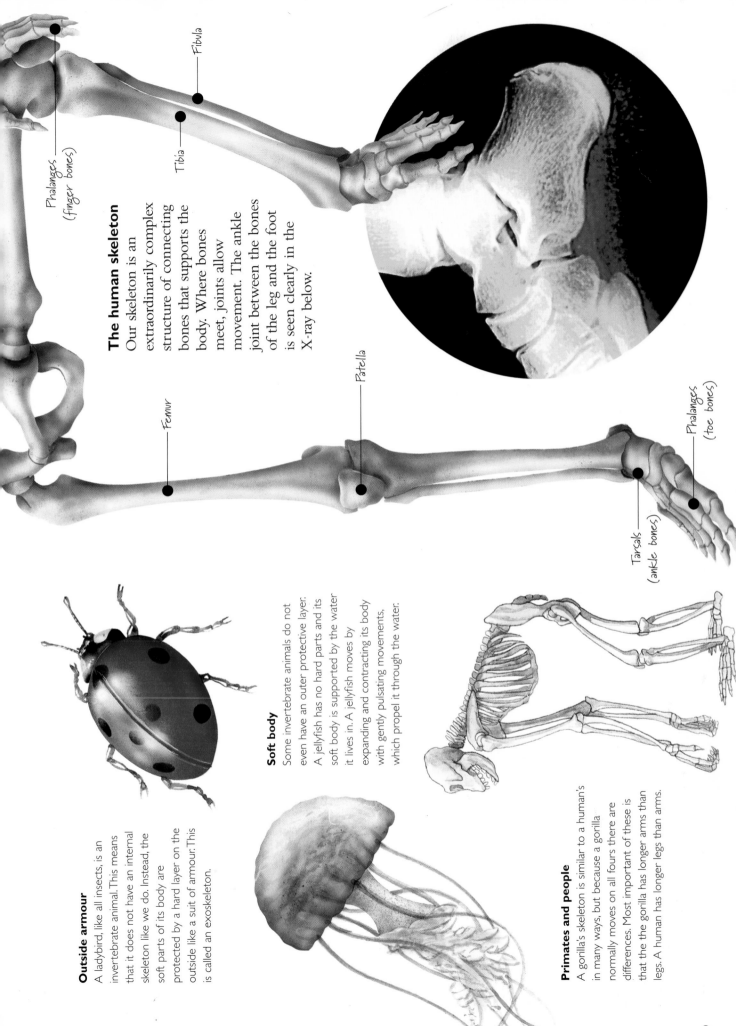

Phalanges
(finger bones)

Fibula

Tibia

The human skeleton

Our skeleton is an extraordinarily complex structure of connecting bones that supports the body. Where bones meet, joints allow movement. The ankle joint between the bones of the leg and the foot is seen clearly in the X-ray below.

Femur

Patella

Phalanges
(toe bones)

Tarsals
(ankle bones)

Outside armour

A ladybird, like all insects, is an invertebrate animal. This means that it does not have an internal skeleton like we do. Instead, the soft parts of its body are protected by a hard layer on the outside like a suit of armour. This is called an exoskeleton.

Soft body

Some invertebrate animals do not even have an outer protective layer. A jellyfish has no hard parts and its soft body is supported by the water it lives in. A jellyfish moves by expanding and contracting its body with gently pulsating movements, which propel it through the water.

Primates and people

A gorilla's skeleton is similar to a human's in many ways, but because a gorilla normally moves on all fours there are differences. Most important of these is that the the gorilla has longer arms than legs. A human has longer legs than arms.

TYPES OF BONES

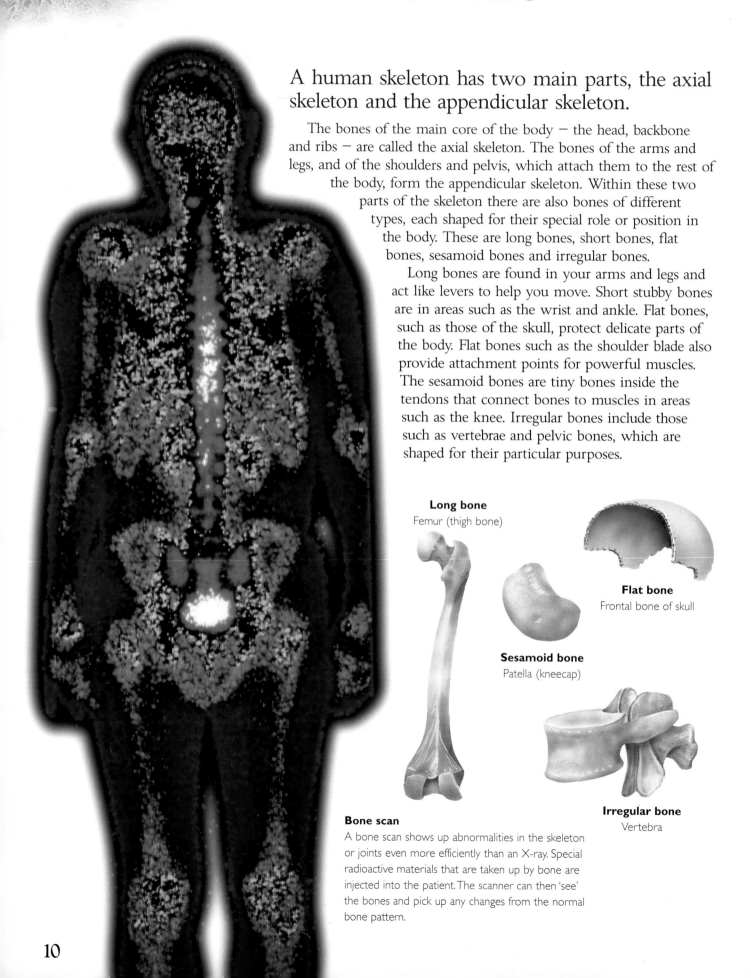

A human skeleton has two main parts, the axial skeleton and the appendicular skeleton.

The bones of the main core of the body – the head, backbone and ribs – are called the axial skeleton. The bones of the arms and legs, and of the shoulders and pelvis, which attach them to the rest of the body, form the appendicular skeleton. Within these two parts of the skeleton there are also bones of different types, each shaped for their special role or position in the body. These are long bones, short bones, flat bones, sesamoid bones and irregular bones.

Long bones are found in your arms and legs and act like levers to help you move. Short stubby bones are in areas such as the wrist and ankle. Flat bones, such as those of the skull, protect delicate parts of the body. Flat bones such as the shoulder blade also provide attachment points for powerful muscles. The sesamoid bones are tiny bones inside the tendons that connect bones to muscles in areas such as the knee. Irregular bones include those such as vertebrae and pelvic bones, which are shaped for their particular purposes.

Long bone
Femur (thigh bone)

Flat bone
Frontal bone of skull

Sesamoid bone
Patella (kneecap)

Irregular bone
Vertebra

Bone scan
A bone scan shows up abnormalities in the skeleton or joints even more efficiently than an X-ray. Special radioactive materials that are taken up by bone are injected into the patient. The scanner can then 'see' the bones and pick up any changes from the normal bone pattern.

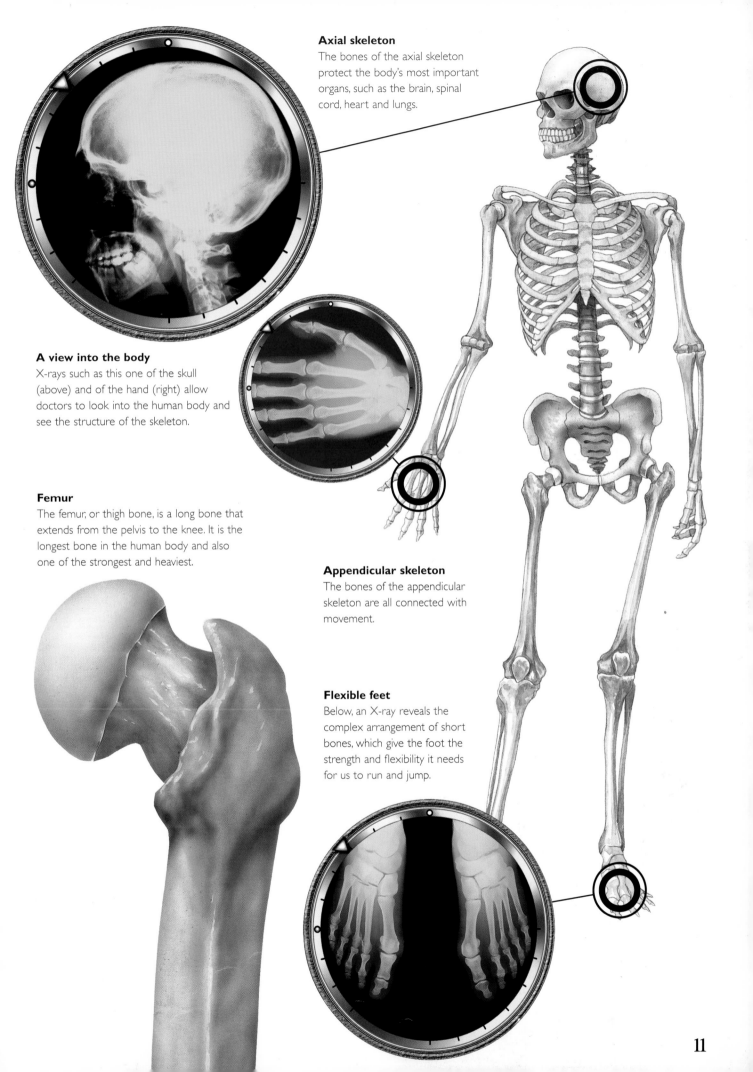

Axial skeleton
The bones of the axial skeleton protect the body's most important organs, such as the brain, spinal cord, heart and lungs.

A view into the body
X-rays such as this one of the skull (above) and of the hand (right) allow doctors to look into the human body and see the structure of the skeleton.

Femur
The femur, or thigh bone, is a long bone that extends from the pelvis to the knee. It is the longest bone in the human body and also one of the strongest and heaviest.

Appendicular skeleton
The bones of the appendicular skeleton are all connected with movement.

Flexible feet
Below, an X-ray reveals the complex arrangement of short bones, which give the foot the strength and flexibility it needs for us to run and jump.

11

INSIDE A BONE

Compact bone
Compact bone is made up of tightly packed rods of bone. A cross-section of one of these rods from compact bone in the thigh is shown in this micrograph.

Fully developed bones are made of mineral salts, water and organic tissues. Within each are two different kinds of bone – compact, and cancellous.

Compact bone is smooth and solid. Cancellous, or spongy, bone has a honeycomb structure so is much lighter than compact bone, but still very strong. A long bone, such as the femur, is a tube of compact bone with cancellous bone inside it. Jellylike marrow fills the centre of the bone and the cavities of the cancellous bone. Flat and irregular bones are made up of thin layers of compact bone around an inner layer of cancellous bone and red bone marrow.

The outer surface of a bone is wrapped in a tough membrane called the periosteum. This protects the bone and provides a surface for tendons and ligaments to attach to. The periosteum covers all of the bone except parts where it joins to other bones. These areas, called joints, are covered with cartilage – a tough, bendy material, which is softer than bone. Periosteum contains lots of blood vessels and nerves, and damage to it causes most of the pain when you fracture a bone.

Inside a long bone
A long bone is made up of an outer layer of compact bone around a layer of spongy bone. A cavity in the centre is filled with bone marrow, which produces red blood cells. At each end of a long bone is more spongy bone, with its honeycomb structure. Blood vessels run through the bones and provide food, oxygen and minerals to keep them healthy.

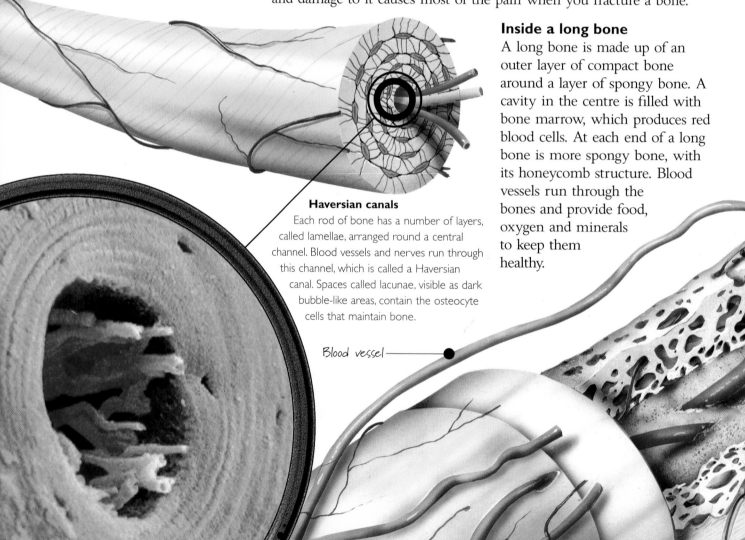

Haversian canals
Each rod of bone has a number of layers, called lamellae, arranged round a central channel. Blood vessels and nerves run through this channel, which is called a Haversian canal. Spaces called lacunae, visible as dark bubble-like areas, contain the osteocyte cells that maintain bone.

Blood vessel

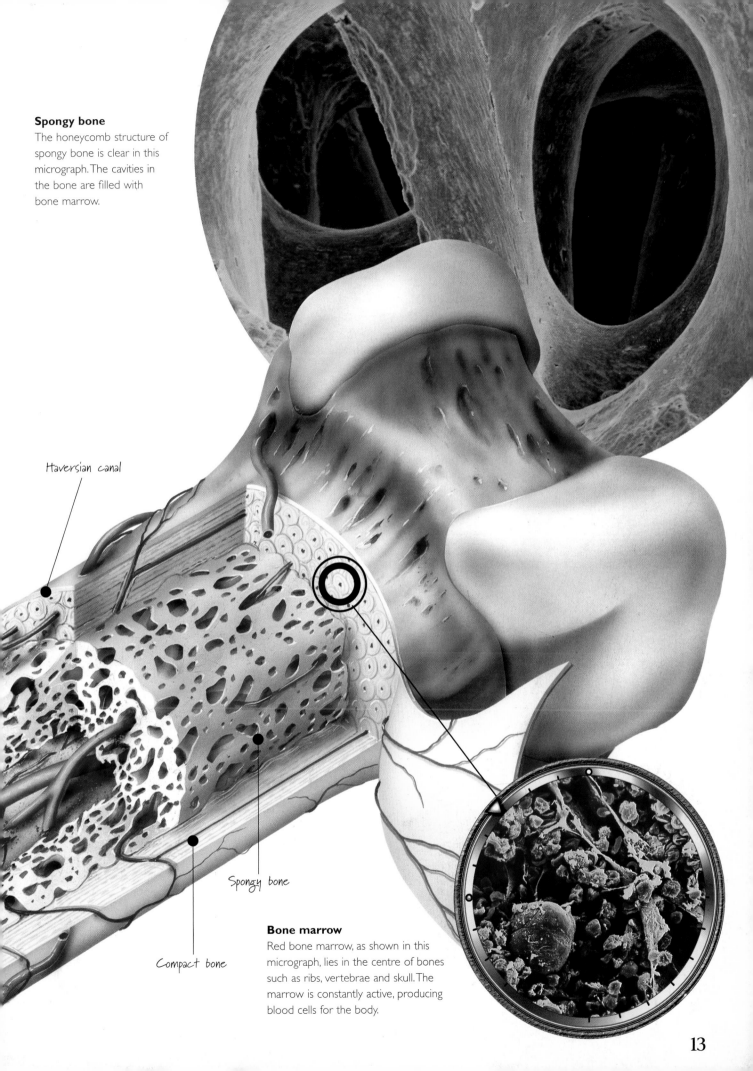

Spongy bone
The honeycomb structure of spongy bone is clear in this micrograph. The cavities in the bone are filled with bone marrow.

Haversian canal

Spongy bone

Compact bone

Bone marrow
Red bone marrow, as shown in this micrograph, lies in the centre of bones such as ribs, vertebrae and skull. The marrow is constantly active, producing blood cells for the body.

13

How Bones Grow

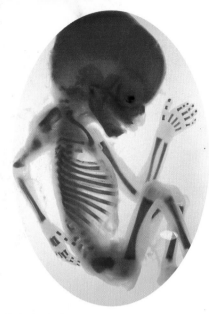

Baby's skeleton
The skeleton shown in this X-ray of a 12-week-old foetus in the womb is made of cartilage, not bone. The body does not have to support weight at this stage so does not need the strength of bone. See how large the baby's head is in relation to its body. Even at birth the head of a baby is about a quarter of its total length. The head of an adult is about one eighth of the total height.

Bones begin to grow when a baby is in the womb and do not completely finish growing until that person is about 25 years old.

Most of the skeleton of a foetus, a baby in the womb, starts as cartilage, a tough, bendy material. When the foetus is about eight weeks old, bone begins to replace cartilage in a process called ossification. Other parts of the skeleton, such as the flat bones at the top of the skull, start as membrane and gradually become bone. But not all of the fully grown skeleton is made from bone. Some of the skeleton stays as cartilage.

Cartilage covers the areas where bones meet at joints, and forms parts of the body such as the trachea or windpipe, the outer part of the ear and the shape of the nose. Push the end of your nose and you will be able to feel the tough, bendy cartilage.

Bendy nose
Much of the nose is shaped of cartilage. This gives the nose flexibility so we can wrinkle it up when we sniff or smell a bad odour. Inside, the nose is divided in half by bone and cartilage.

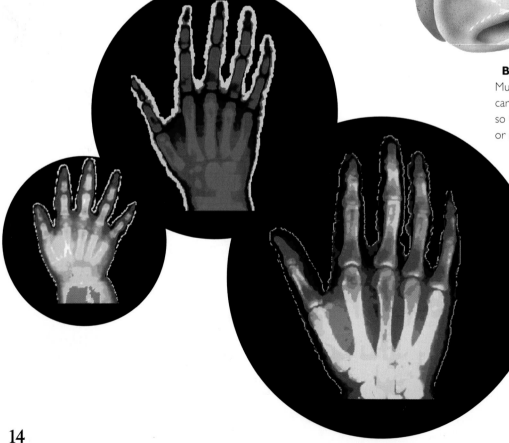

A growing hand
Colour X-rays show the development of the bones of the hand from a toddler to a fully grown adult. In the two-year-old (far left) there are still large areas of cartilage, showing up here as spaces between the bones. These areas gradually become bone, until in the hand of the adult the bones are all fully developed and meet at the joints.

Ears

The outer ears are sculpted in cartilage, which is strong yet flexible. The ears can be pushed out or squashed flat against your head, but they quickly spring back to shape.

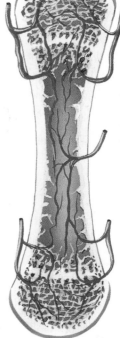

Pierced cartilage

Some people like to have strong cartilage pierced so they can wear rings in the upper part of the ear or the nose.

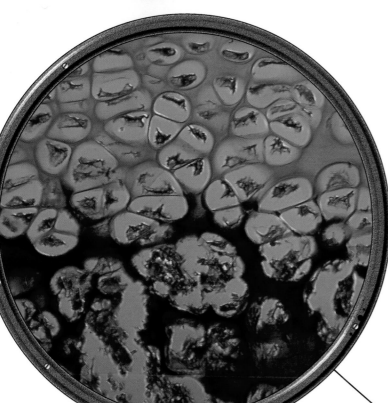

Growing bone

This micrograph of a foot bone of a human embryo shows the beginning of ossification – the process of replacing cartilage with bone. The area at the top of the picture has become bone and ossification is gradually spreading towards the bottom of the picture.

Ossification

Ossification, the process of replacing cartilage with bone, begins while a baby is still in the womb. Cartilage consists of cartilage cells, called chondroblasts, embedded in a tough jelly. When the baby's cartilage skeleton begins to grow and change into bone, groups of a new type of cell, called osteoblasts, grow in the middle of the cartilage and produce bone in the same shape. Bone is made of osteocytes, cells derived from osteoblasts, embedded in a rigid material made of calcium phosphate.

15

THE SKULL — CRANIUM

The skull is made up of 28 bones that can be divided into two main areas — the cranium and the face, which includes the ear bones.

The bones of the skull surround the brain and the sense organs and give structure to the face. The top of the skull, called the cranium, makes a bony box around the brain. The eight bones that make up the cranium are joined tightly together at joints called sutures. These have irregular edges and fit together like the pieces of a jigsaw. The joints do not move and their jagged shape makes them stronger than if the bones joined with straight edges.

When a baby is born the bones of the cranium are not completely joined but held together by a membrane. These 'soft spots' allow the skull to be squeezed slightly during birth.

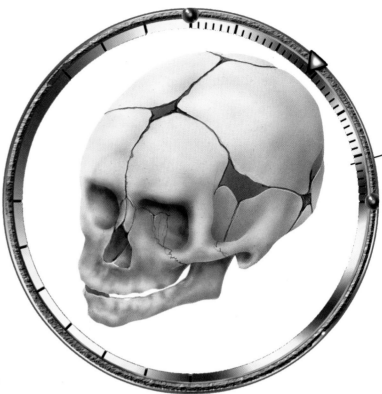

Soft spots
The soft areas between the bones of a baby's cranium are called fontanelles. The bones gradually knit together until they are completely joined by the time the baby is about 18 months old.

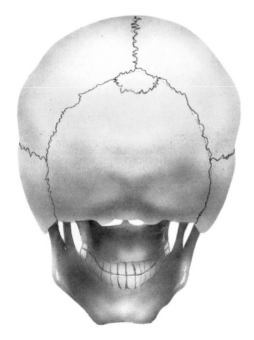

Back of the head
The sides and roof of the skull are formed by the large curving parietal bones. Below these is the occipital bone, which forms the base of the back of the head. Together these bones form a strong protective case.

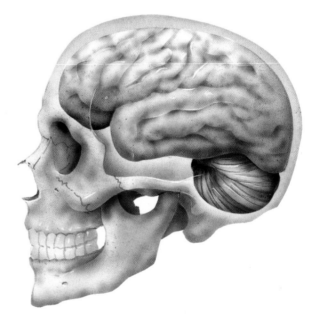

Brain box
The bones of the top of the skull keep the brain protected from knocks and damage. A big head or large forehead doesn't mean you are extra brainy.

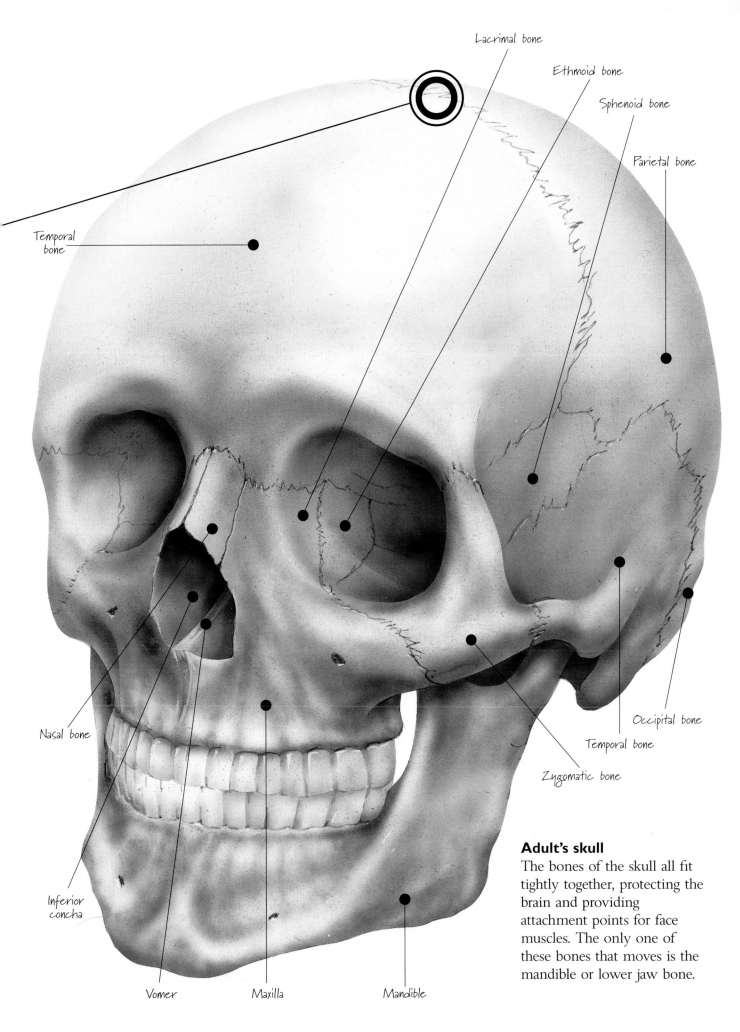

Lacrimal bone

Ethmoid bone

Sphenoid bone

Parietal bone

Temporal bone

Nasal bone

Inferior concha

Vomer

Maxilla

Mandible

Occipital bone

Temporal bone

Zygomatic bone

Adult's skull

The bones of the skull all fit tightly together, protecting the brain and providing attachment points for face muscles. The only one of these bones that moves is the mandible or lower jaw bone.

17

THE SKULL – FACE BONES

The face is made up of 14 bones which give the face its shape. Face bones also form part of the eye sockets and nose cavity and provide sturdy attachment points for teeth and muscles.

It is easy to feel the bones of your face with your fingers. The lower jaw bone is the largest bone in the face and the only one you can move. It is the movements of this bone, up and down and from side to side, which allow us to chew. The upper jaw bone does not move. As well as the 14 bones in the head there are three bones in each ear – the malleus, incus and stapes. The malleus is attached to the eardrum and picks up vibrations caused by sound waves. These vibrations are passed on to the other bones and to the rest of the hearing apparatus, where they are turned into nerve signals and passed to the brain.

Eye sockets

The eyes are held in place in bony sockets called orbits. The top of the orbits is formed by the frontal bone and the bottom by the zygomatic, or cheek, bones.

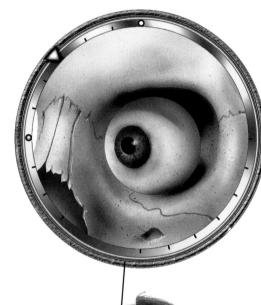

Ear bones

The bones of the ear, called the auditory ossicles, are the smallest in the body. The stapes - also known as the stirrup because of its shape - is only about 3 millimetres (⅛ inch) long.

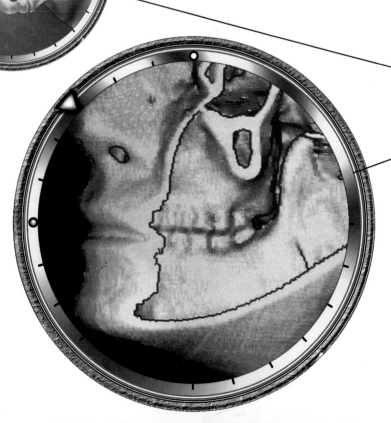

Moulding the face

Bones give the face its structure and their shape makes one face different from another. The lower jaw bone, the mandible (left), is the strongest bone in the face.

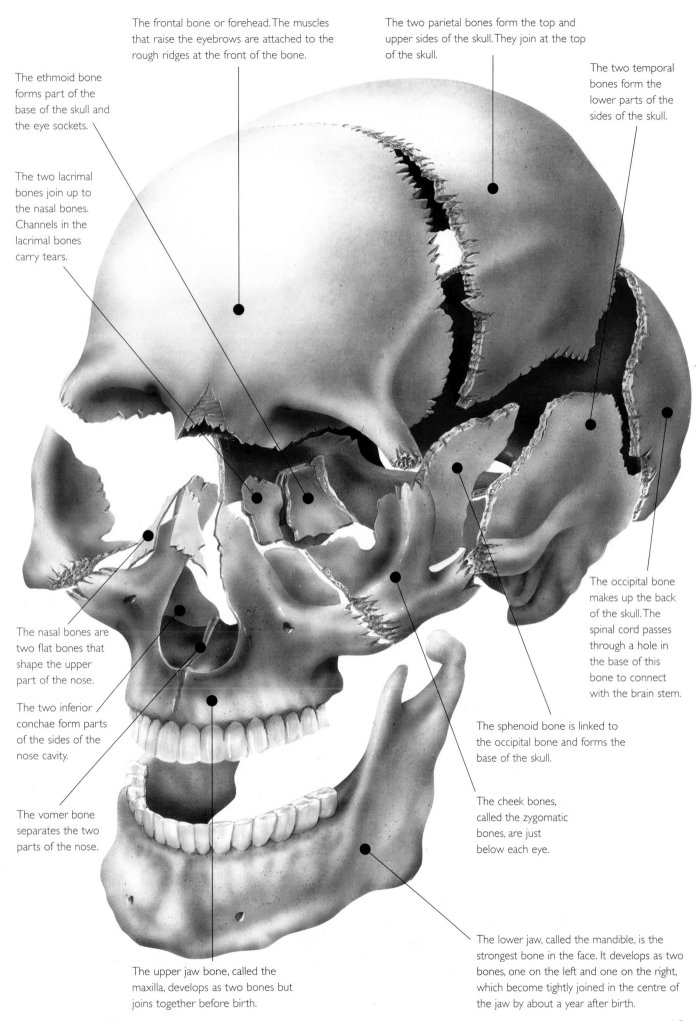

The frontal bone or forehead. The muscles that raise the eyebrows are attached to the rough ridges at the front of the bone.

The two parietal bones form the top and upper sides of the skull. They join at the top of the skull.

The two temporal bones form the lower parts of the sides of the skull.

The ethmoid bone forms part of the base of the skull and the eye sockets.

The two lacrimal bones join up to the nasal bones. Channels in the lacrimal bones carry tears.

The occipital bone makes up the back of the skull. The spinal cord passes through a hole in the base of this bone to connect with the brain stem.

The nasal bones are two flat bones that shape the upper part of the nose.

The two inferior conchae form parts of the sides of the nose cavity.

The vomer bone separates the two parts of the nose.

The sphenoid bone is linked to the occipital bone and forms the base of the skull.

The cheek bones, called the zygomatic bones, are just below each eye.

The lower jaw, called the mandible, is the strongest bone in the face. It develops as two bones, one on the left and one on the right, which become tightly joined in the centre of the jaw by about a year after birth.

The upper jaw bone, called the maxilla, develops as two bones but joins together before birth.

The spine

Vertebrae are made of spongy, or cancellous, bone surrounded by a layer of compact bone.

THE SPINE

The spine, also called the backbone, is the central support of the back of the body. It is made up of a series of separate irregular bones called vertebrae.

Although each of these can move only a small amount, the movements of all the vertebrae together make the spine extremely flexible. We can bend double to touch our toes, lean over backwards and curl our back right round. There are 26 vertebrae in all. First are the seven cervical vertebrae, then 12 thoracic vertebrae and five lumbar vertebrae. Below these are the sacrum and the coccyx. The sacrum is part of the pelvis and is made up of five bones joined together. The coccyx, made up of four joined bones, is the only remnant of a tail in humans. The three types of vertebrae are slightly different shapes but all have a similar structure.

At the front of a vertebra is a round, solid shape, called the body, and behind this is a bony tube. On the tube are bony fins called neural spines to which muscles are attached. The bony tubes of all the vertebrae link up to make a channel through which the spinal cord passes. The spinal cord extends from the brain down most of the spine, and nerves from the spinal cord connect with every part of the body. In between each vertebra are discs of cartilage, which keep the bones from grinding against each other. About a quarter of an adult's spine is made of cartilage.

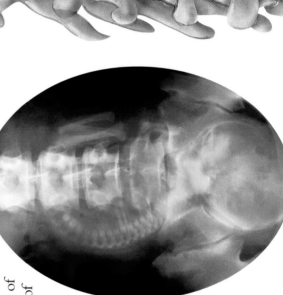

Baby's spine

The C-shaped spine of a baby in the womb is made of cartilage, so it is soft and very flexible. This curved spine allows the baby to fit snugly in the womb, with its head almost touching its knees. The mother's spine and pelvis are also visible in this micrograph.

The backbone

The spine is arranged in a series of alternating curves, which help to balance the human body on two legs. In most other mammals the skeleton is designed to be a horizontal support. The curves make the spine much stronger and more stable than if it were just a straight line.

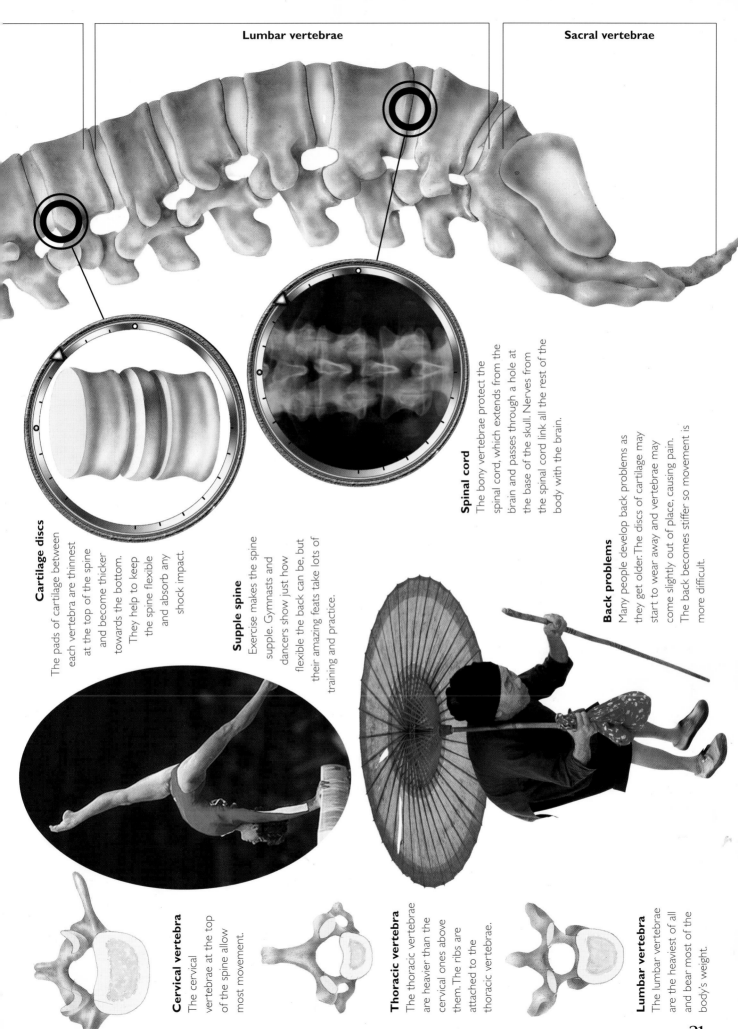

Cartilage discs

The pads of cartilage between each vertebra are thinnest at the top of the spine and become thicker towards the bottom. They help to keep the spine flexible and absorb any shock impact.

Supple spine

Exercise makes the spine supple. Gymnasts and dancers show just how flexible the back can be, but their amazing feats take lots of training and practice.

Spinal cord

The bony vertebrae protect the spinal cord, which extends from the brain and passes through a hole at the base of the skull. Nerves from the spinal cord link all the rest of the body with the brain.

Back problems

Many people develop back problems as they get older. The discs of cartilage may start to wear away and vertebrae may come slightly out of place, causing pain. The back becomes stiffer so movement is more difficult.

Cervical vertebra

The cervical vertebrae at the top of the spine allow most movement.

Thoracic vertebra

The thoracic vertebrae are heavier than the cervical ones above them. The ribs are attached to the thoracic vertebrae.

Lumbar vertebra

The lumbar vertebrae are the heaviest of all and bear most of the body's weight.

21

Ribs

Tap the middle of your chest and you will feel your breastbone, called the sternum. It is a flat bone, which is about 15 centimetres (6 inches) long in an adult and made of spongy, or cancellous bone, enclosed by two layers of compact bone.

Linked to this bone are the ribs, which curve round from the spine to the front of your body. These form a bony framework, known as the thoracic cage, which protects your chest. Most people have 12 pairs of ribs. They are flat, curved bones, linked to the vertebrae of the spine at the back of the body. At the front they are joined to the breastbone by bands of cartilage. These slender bars of bone and cartilage are far more flexible than a shield of solid bone would be. This is vital for breathing as the rib cage has to be able to expand as you take air into the lungs.

Bony cage

The breastbone and ribs, which make up the bones of the chest, combine strength with flexibility.

Breastbone

Rib

Protective cage

The ribs and breastbone protect the organs of the chest, including the heart and lungs, from knocks and injury. The lower part of the gullet is also protected by the ribs.

True ribs

The first seven pairs of ribs (counting from the top, right) are called true ribs. At the front of the body they are linked directly to the breastbone by bands of cartilage. At the back they are attached to the thoracic vertebrae.

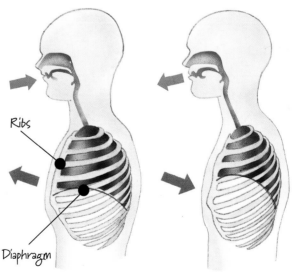

Ribs

Diaphragm

Breathing in   **Breathing out**

Taking a breath

When you breathe in, the diaphragm flattens and muscles called intercostals lift the ribs upwards and outwards, allowing the lungs to get bigger as air flows into them. When you breathe out again, the diaphragm and ribs relax, and the lungs contract as air flows out.

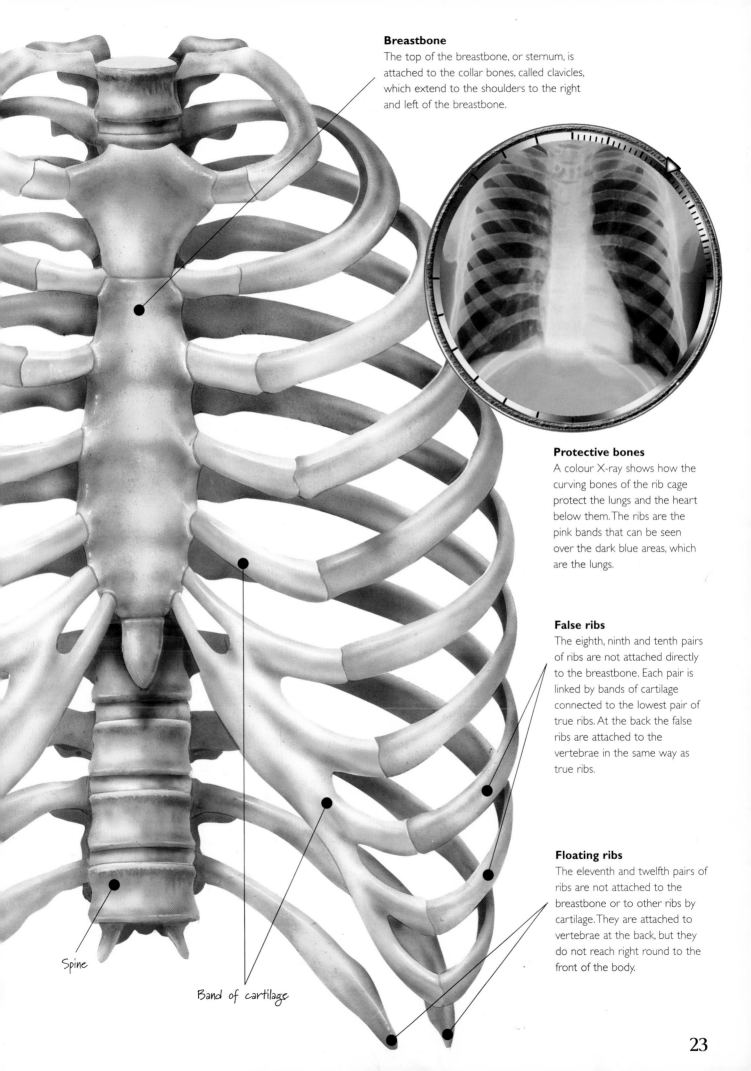

Breastbone
The top of the breastbone, or sternum, is attached to the collar bones, called clavicles, which extend to the shoulders to the right and left of the breastbone.

Protective bones
A colour X-ray shows how the curving bones of the rib cage protect the lungs and the heart below them. The ribs are the pink bands that can be seen over the dark blue areas, which are the lungs.

False ribs
The eighth, ninth and tenth pairs of ribs are not attached directly to the breastbone. Each pair is linked by bands of cartilage connected to the lowest pair of true ribs. At the back the false ribs are attached to the vertebrae in the same way as true ribs.

Floating ribs
The eleventh and twelfth pairs of ribs are not attached to the breastbone or to other ribs by cartilage. They are attached to vertebrae at the back, but they do not reach right round to the front of the body.

Spine

Band of cartilage

23

SHOULDER, ARM & HAND

A delicate touch
The complex structure of the human hand allows humans to make more delicate, precise movements than any other creatures.

The bones of the shoulder, arm and hand are amazingly flexible.

The shoulder joint allows the arms a much greater range of movement than the hip joints give the legs, because the arms do not have to support the weight of the body like the legs do. The structure of the hand provides both great strength and the ability to make the finest, most precise movements.

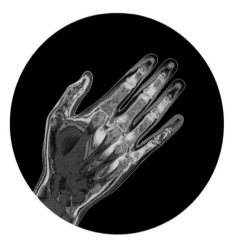

Inside the hand
A coloured X-ray reveals the bones of the hand. Each hand contains 27 separate bones, linked together with muscles and tendons.

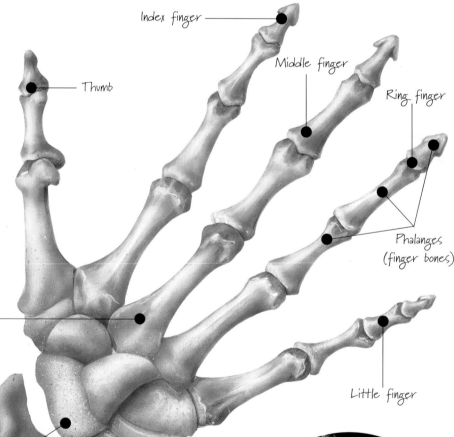

Index finger

Thumb

Middle finger

Ring finger

Phalanges (finger bones)

Metacarpals (hand bones)

Little finger

The bones of the hand
The bones of the hand are called the metacarpals, and the bones of the fingers, the phalanges. There are three phalanges in each finger and two in the thumb. At the wrist are eight small bones called the carpals. These support the muscles that move the fingers and thumb.

Carpals (wrist bones)

Karate blow
A karate expert can break a piece of wood with one blow of his hand, showing just how strong bone is. Karate needs lots of training and very special movements, so don't try this yourself.

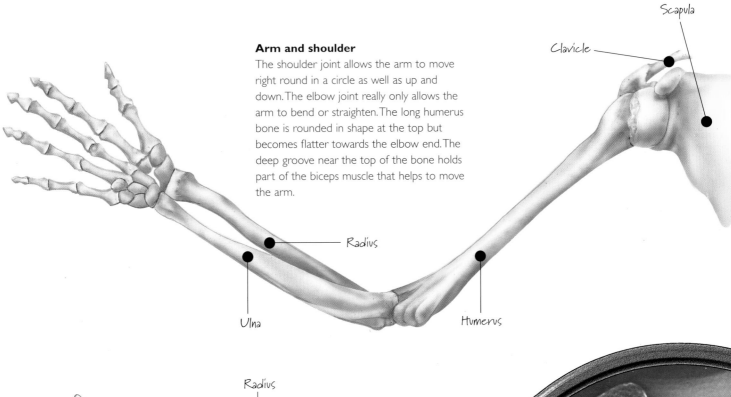

Arm and shoulder

The shoulder joint allows the arm to move right round in a circle as well as up and down. The elbow joint really only allows the arm to bend or straighten. The long humerus bone is rounded in shape at the top but becomes flatter towards the elbow end. The deep groove near the top of the bone holds part of the biceps muscle that helps to move the arm.

Radius

Ulna

Humerus

Scapula

Clavicle

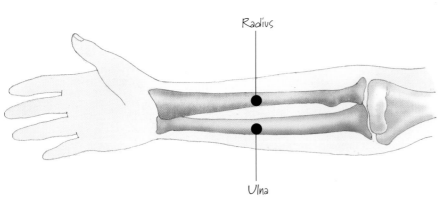

Radius

Ulna

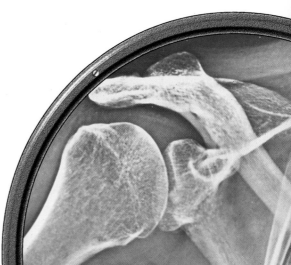

Radius and ulna

The bones of the lower arm, the radius and ulna, link with the humerus at the elbow and with the carpals at the wrist. A membrane lies between them. When the arm is hanging down with the palm of the hand facing forwards, the two bones are parallel to each other. But in order to turn the palm over, the bones move so that the radius crosses in front of the ulna, twisting the wrist.

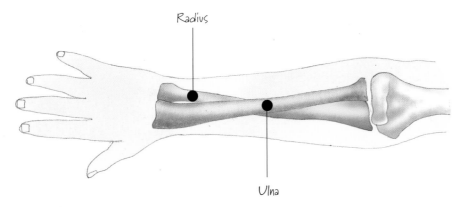

Radius

Ulna

Shoulder bones

The bones of the shoulder – the collar bone, or clavicle, and the shoulder blade, or scapula – can be seen in this X-ray. The upper arm bone, the humerus, is linked to the shoulder blade by a ball and socket joint.

25

HIP BONES

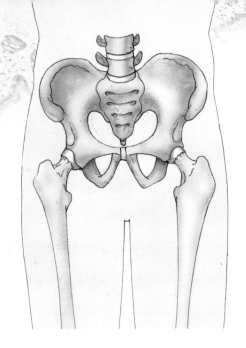

The hips support much of the body's weight and help us stand upright and move. Each hip is made up of three bones, which are separate at birth but become joined into one as you grow up. These bones are the ilium, ischium and pubis.

The big bone that you can feel at the side of your body, just below the waist, is the ilium and below this is the pubis. The ischium is at the back, in your bottom. The ilium joins to the sacrum at the base of the spine. Together the hip bones and the sacrum make a basin-like structure called the pelvis. The bones of the pelvis help to protect some of the soft inside parts of the body, such as the intestines and, in women, the womb. The large muscles that move the thighs are attached to the broad, flat shape of the ilium.

Body support
The basin-shaped human pelvis sits beneath the backbone and helps support the body on two legs, leaving the arms free for jobs other than moving around.

An inside look
The bones of an adult pelvis are shown in this micrograph. At the lower right of the picture is the rounded head of the thigh bone fitting neatly into the socket of the pelvis.

New hip
If the joint between the hip and the top of the femur is damaged by an accident or worn away in old age, it can be replaced in a special operation. A new rounded head of stainless steel is fitted to the femur and a cup of steel or plastic placed in the hip bone.

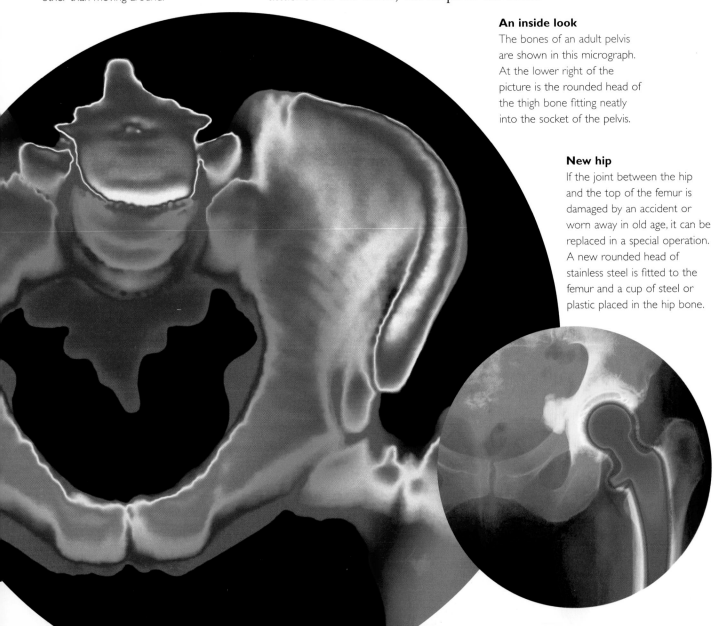

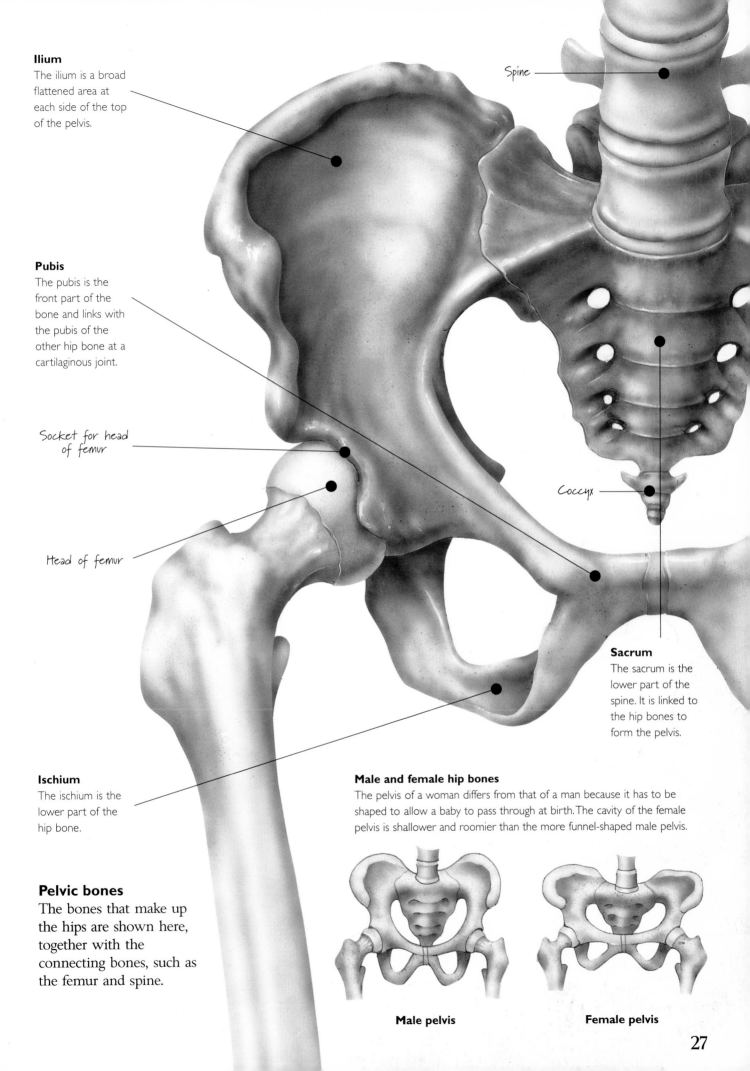

Ilium
The ilium is a broad flattened area at each side of the top of the pelvis.

Spine

Pubis
The pubis is the front part of the bone and links with the pubis of the other hip bone at a cartilaginous joint.

Socket for head of femur

Coccyx

Head of femur

Sacrum
The sacrum is the lower part of the spine. It is linked to the hip bones to form the pelvis.

Ischium
The ischium is the lower part of the hip bone.

Male and female hip bones
The pelvis of a woman differs from that of a man because it has to be shaped to allow a baby to pass through at birth. The cavity of the female pelvis is shallower and roomier than the more funnel-shaped male pelvis.

Pelvic bones
The bones that make up the hips are shown here, together with the connecting bones, such as the femur and spine.

Male pelvis

Female pelvis

LEG & FOOT

Unlike most other mammals, humans have leg and foot bones designed for standing upright and walking on two legs, not four.

The main part of the leg has three bones. The thigh bone, called the femur, extends from the hip joint to the knee and is the longest, strongest bone in the body. Below the knee are two other long bones – the shin bone, called the tibia, which you can feel at the front of your lower leg, and the fibula. At the kneecap is a further bone called the patella. This sits in the tendon of the muscle that straightens the leg.

There are 26 bones in each foot – one less than in each hand. In the ankle are seven tarsal bones (the wrist has eight bones). The main body of the foot is made up of the metatarsals. The toes, like the fingers, have 14 bones, called phalanges. The arched structure of the foot helps to spread the body's weight.

Tibia
The tibia is the larger of the two lower leg bones. It helps to support the body's weight.

Inside the foot
A coloured X-ray shows the arrangement of the 26 bones of the foot.

Feet on the ground
The bones of the toes are shorter and fatter than those of the fingers to help us balance as we stand on two legs. The big toe cannot be opposed against the other toes like the thumb can against the fingers.

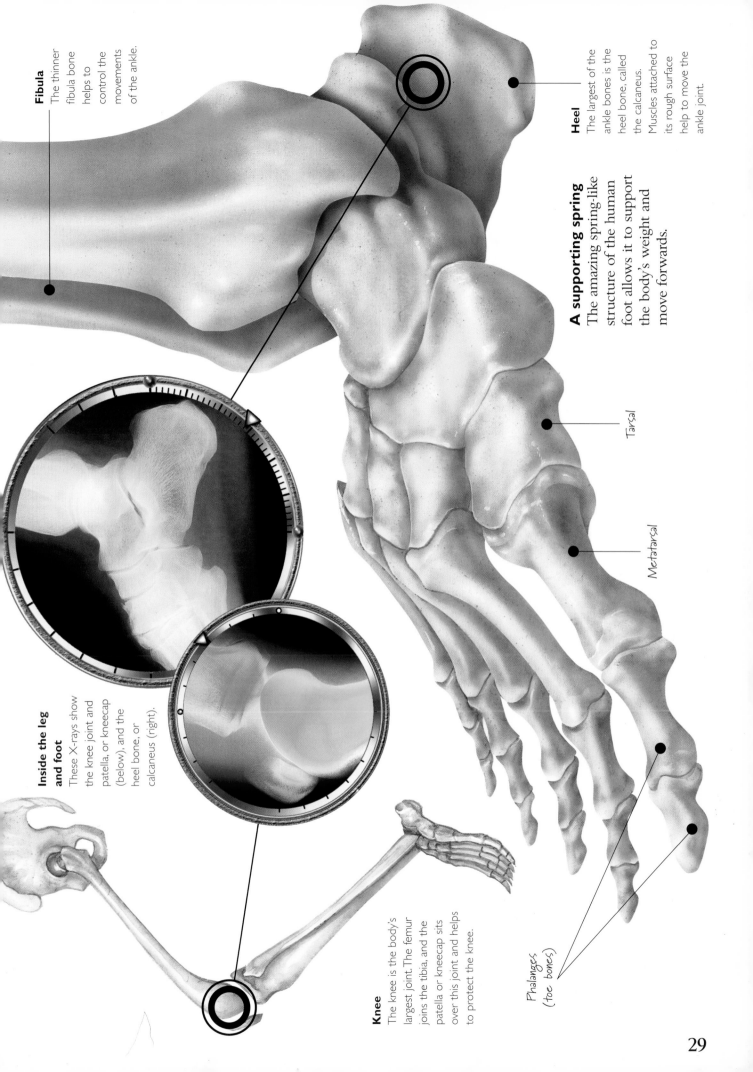

Fibula

The thinner fibula bone helps to control the movements of the ankle.

Heel

The largest of the ankle bones is the heel bone, called the calcaneus. Muscles attached to its rough surface help to move the ankle joint.

A supporting spring

The amazing spring-like structure of the human foot allows it to support the body's weight and move forwards.

Tarsal

Metatarsal

Inside the leg and foot

These X-rays show the knee joint and patella, or kneecap (below), and the heel bone, or calcaneus (right).

Knee

The knee is the body's largest joint. The femur joins the tibia, and the patella or kneecap sits over this joint and helps to protect the knee.

Phalanges (toe bones)

29

MOVEMENT

Pincer movements

The human hand is capable of such fine movements that we can pick up an object the size of a pinhead between thumb and forefinger.

The human body is capable of an extraordinary range of movements, from simply gripping something between thumb and finger to the coordinated actions necessary to run, jump or ride a bicycle.

Muscles, bones and joints work together to bring about movements. Muscles are attached to bones. When a muscle contracts, or gets shorter, it pulls the bone it is attached to and makes it move at the joint. The bone is like a lever to which the muscle applies force. Many of the movements we make, such as walking, we don't need to think about. Others, such as those required in many sports or for playing a musical instrument, require training and practice.

Cycling

Cycling demands the coordination of lots of muscles in the lower and upper body to power the bicycle and keep your balance.

Running and jumping

Hurdling, in which athletes race round a track and jump small fences called hurdles (right), demands considerable strength and flexibility. The ball and socket joint at the hip allows the leg to be lifted at the side of the body.

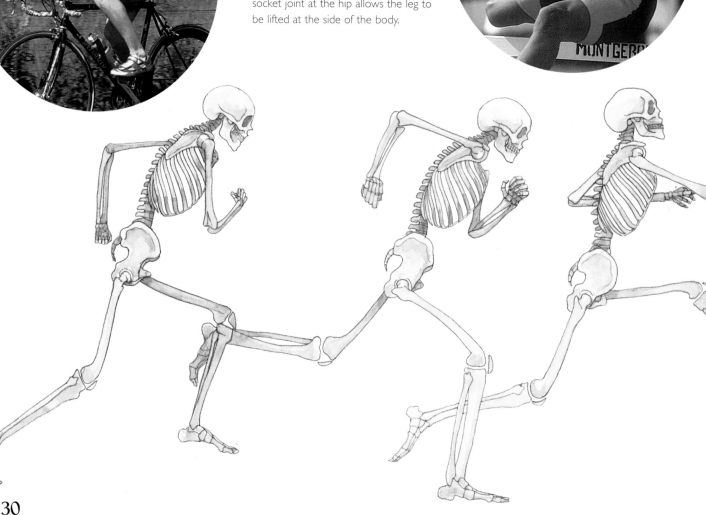

How the arm works

The human arm works much like the series of levers that operate a mechanical grabber. Muscles on the upper arm pull on the bone to raise it from the elbow. The hand can bend forward at the wrist and the complex arrangement of bones and joints in the hand enable it to grip any object.

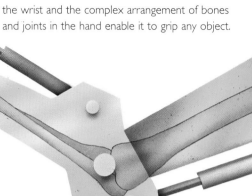

Body coordination

Table tennis demands skill and precise coordination between the eye and the movements of the arm and hand to place the ball correctly.

Moving through water

Swimming strokes use the arms and legs to push the body through the water. Swimming is one of the best body exercises.

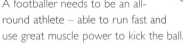

The flexible shoulder

The shoulder joint is the most mobile of all. This allows us to make movements that demand flexibility and strength, such as swinging a baseball bat to hit a ball.

Muscle power

A footballer needs to be an all-round athlete – able to run fast and use great muscle power to kick the ball.

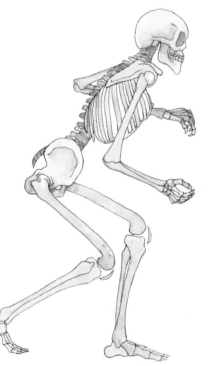

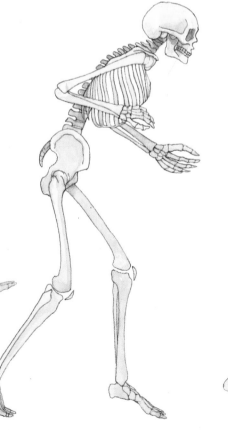

On the move

Our bodies are designed for movement. We walk, run and jump, with barely a thought for all the muscles and bones inside the body that power our actions. Plenty of activity helps keep the bones and muscles healthy and in good working order.

JOINTS

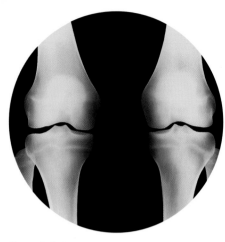

Knee joints
The joints between the femur, or thigh bone, and tibia, or lower leg bone, are shown in this micrograph. The kneecap, or patella, is visible as a yellow area near the head of each femur.

A joint is a place where two or more bones meet. Hip joints and shoulder joints are among those that move freely. Others, such as the cartilaginous joints between vertebrae, have limited movement, but at some there is no movement at all.

The bones of the skull meet with fixed joints, which do not move. Joints that move freely are called synovial joints. There are many different types, including ball and socket joints, hinge joints and gliding joints. Although they all move in slightly different ways, they have some features in common.

The ends of the bones meeting at synovial joints are covered with a thin layer of cartilage. This protects the bones and stops them grinding against each other. Lining or covering parts of the joint is a synovial membrane. This secretes a sticky liquid called synovial fluid, which oils the joint and helps to keep it healthy.

In some joints there are also little sacs of fluid called bursae. These cushion the joint and help a tendon or ligament, for example, glide over a bone. Ligaments are stretchy fibrous strips, which hold bones together at joints and keep them from moving too far apart.

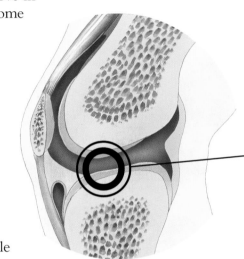

Cartilaginous covering
The ends of bones that meet at joints are covered with a thin layer of cartilage. In this cutaway of a knee joint, the cartilage covering on the femur and tibia is shown.

The top of the skull
The bones at the top of the skull are not joined when a baby is born, but they gradually knit together by the time a child is about 18 months old.

Fixed joint
Once the bones of the skull have knitted together, they fit tightly at jigsaw-like joins and there is no movement between them. Fibrous tissue between the bones draws the bones together.

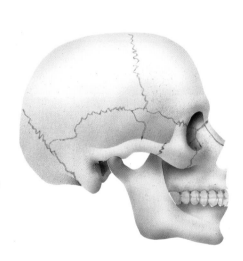

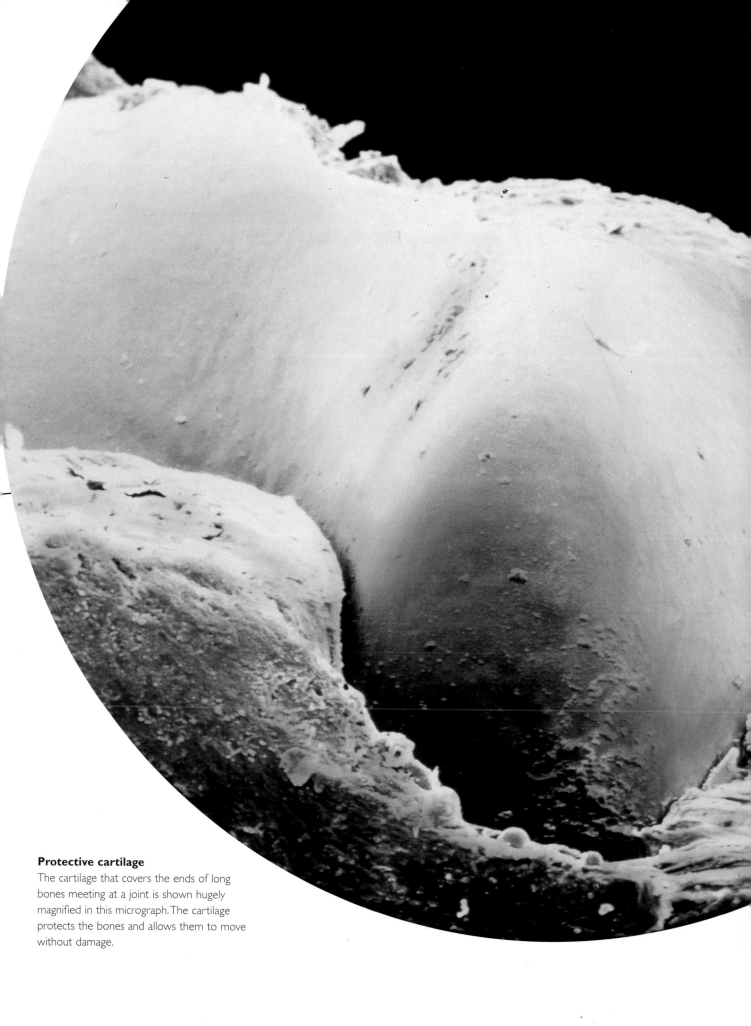

Protective cartilage
The cartilage that covers the ends of long bones meeting at a joint is shown hugely magnified in this micrograph. The cartilage protects the bones and allows them to move without damage.

HINGE JOINTS

Hinge joint
A hinge joint allows movement in one plane, just like the hinge on a door.

A hinge joint allows the linked parts of the body to be bent or extended. Hinged joints include those at the elbow, knee, ankle and the joints between the fingers.

For example, the arm can be bent at the elbow, by the actions of the biceps and brachialis muscles, or extended with the triceps muscle. The knee works in a similar way, but it is a more complex joint because it can also swivel slightly as you walk. Injuries to the knee are common — jogging on hard pavements puts too much stress on the knee and can damage cartilage, and athletes often strain the hamstring muscles at the back of the leg that enable the knee to flex.

Bending the arm
A simple action, such as bending your arm, depends on the efficient action of the hinge joint at the elbow and all the ligaments, muscles and tendons that help it move. Holding the plate with a bent arm gives a much steadier support than if the arm was held out straight. Hinge joints in the fingers allow you to grip tightly.

Skier's knee
Sports such as skiing cause strain to the knee joints. The constant bending of the knee required in skiing puts a great deal of pressure on the joint and can twist the knee.

A firm grip
The flexible joints of the fingers allow the human hand to hold on to objects very tightly. This gives the firm grip needed to control, for example, a bicycle's handlebars.

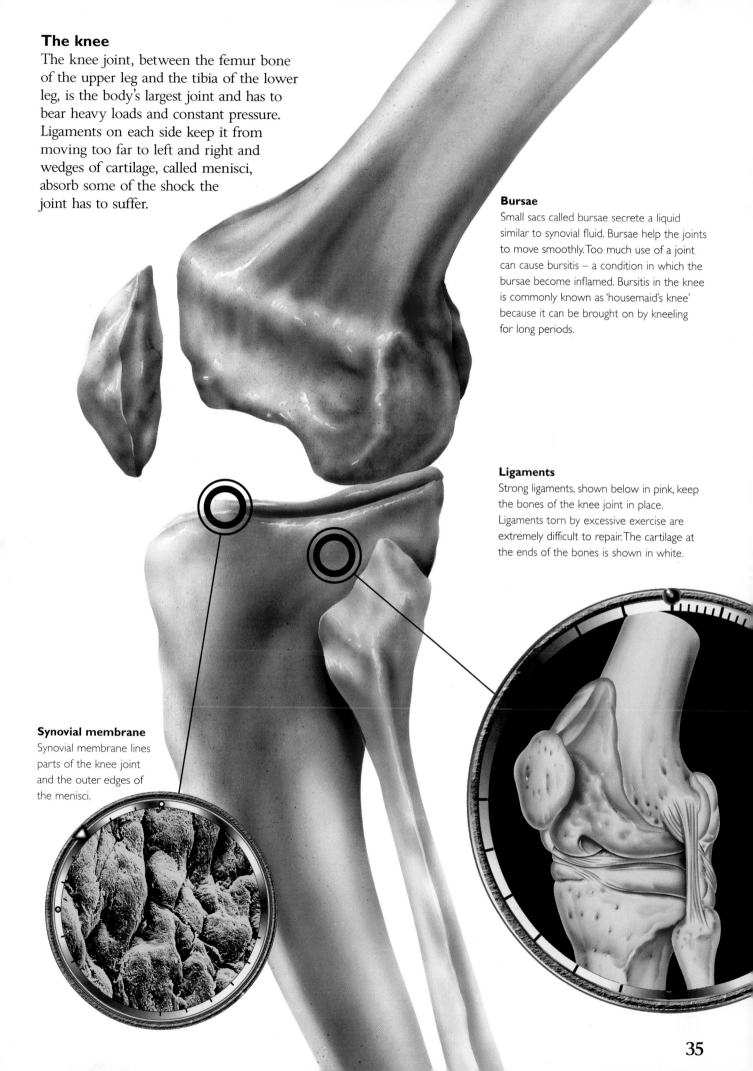

The knee

The knee joint, between the femur bone of the upper leg and the tibia of the lower leg, is the body's largest joint and has to bear heavy loads and constant pressure. Ligaments on each side keep it from moving too far to left and right and wedges of cartilage, called menisci, absorb some of the shock the joint has to suffer.

Bursae

Small sacs called bursae secrete a liquid similar to synovial fluid. Bursae help the joints to move smoothly. Too much use of a joint can cause bursitis – a condition in which the bursae become inflamed. Bursitis in the knee is commonly known as 'housemaid's knee' because it can be brought on by kneeling for long periods.

Ligaments

Strong ligaments, shown below in pink, keep the bones of the knee joint in place. Ligaments torn by excessive exercise are extremely difficult to repair. The cartilage at the ends of the bones is shown in white.

Synovial membrane

Synovial membrane lines parts of the knee joint and the outer edges of the menisci.

BALL & SOCKET JOINTS

Ball and socket joints are the most freely moving of all the joints in the human body. One of the bones that meet at the joint has a rounded head, the ball, which sits snugly in a hollow in the other bone, the socket.

Ball and socket
The ball, or rounded top, of one bone sits neatly inside a cup-like hollow in another, allowing movement in several directions as shown.

The two bones are held together by strong ligaments. A ball and socket joint allows lots of twisting and turning movements but is still very strong. In the shoulder joint, the bone of the upper arm, the humerus, fits into a shallow cup in the shoulder blade. The shoulder joint allows a great range of movement, but, because of this, is easy to dislocate. This happens when the bones are moved too far and the ball comes out of its socket. A dislocated shoulder joint can be slipped back into place by expert manipulation from the outside of the body. The joint of the hip and upper leg is also a ball and socket but it does not allow as much movement as the shoulder joint.

Agile gymnast
The ball and socket joint is amazingly strong as well as flexible, as demonstrated in the position of this gymnast, who is supporting the weight of his whole body on one arm.

Tennis ace
The mobile shoulder joint allows the arm to be moved right round and back with great force as a tennis player returns the ball.

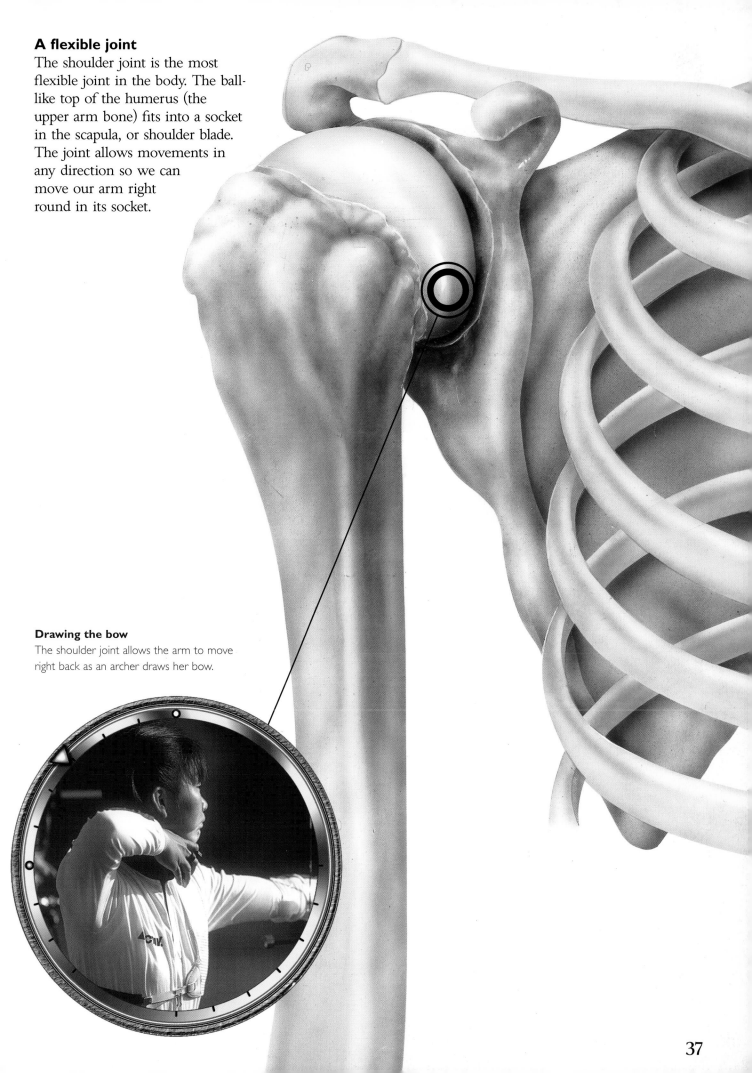

A flexible joint

The shoulder joint is the most flexible joint in the body. The ball-like top of the humerus (the upper arm bone) fits into a socket in the scapula, or shoulder blade. The joint allows movements in any direction so we can move our arm right round in its socket.

Drawing the bow
The shoulder joint allows the arm to move right back as an archer draws her bow.

OTHER JOINTS

Gliding joint

Gliding joints link the tarsal bones in the foot and the carpal bones in the wrist. Two flat bones slide over one another to allow small movements in different directions.

There are many other types of freely moving, or synovial, joints in the body, each allowing a different type of action.

The saddle joint in the thumb, for example, allows the thumb to move up and down and swivel right round. Gliding joints link the tarsal bones in the foot and the carpal bones in the wrist and allow small movements in any direction.

A condyloid joint links the base of the skull to the spine and allows the head to nod. Below this is the pivot joint, which allows you to turn your head and look back over your shoulder.

Condyloid joint

Condyloid joints in the knuckles between the metacarpal bones of the hand and the phalanges of the fingers allow you to bend your hand and fingers and grip tightly.

Saddle joint

The saddle joint, which joins the thumb to the hand, allows such flexibility that you can touch your thumb to the tips of any of your fingers. Both bones have saddle-shaped ends, which fit neatly together, and the joint can make movements in two directions. This joint gives humans the ability to perform many delicate actions with the fingers and thumb.

Delicate but strong

The complex bone structure and different joints of the hand (shown in this X-ray) work together to allow us an enormous range of movements. The hands can make the most delicate actions as well as having great strength.

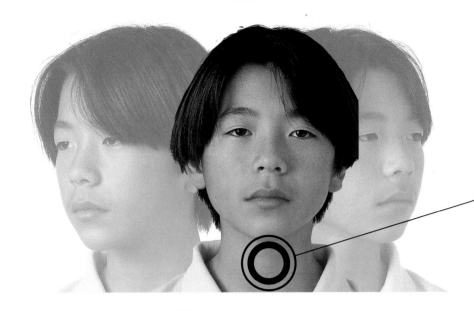

Pivot joint
A pivot joint allows movement around the axis of the joint.

Neck bones
The seven bones in the neck, the cervical vertebrae, are shown in this X-ray. The joint between the top vertebra and the base of the skull is the condyloid. The joint between the first and second vertebrae is the pivot.

Nodding and shaking
A condyloid joint links the skull to the spine and allows the head to be nodded. Below the condyloid joint is a pivot joint which allows the head to swivel round.

Condyloid joint
This is similar to a ball and socket joint but does not allow as much movement.

FRACTURED BONES

Bone is living material and, although it is very strong and can take a lot of strain, it is sometimes injured in a bad fall or other accident.

A break in a bone is called a fracture. In a simple fracture the bone breaks cleanly in one place but does not pierce the skin. If part of the broken bone does come through the skin, this is called a compound fracture. A bone broken in more than one place is a comminuted fracture.

Broken bones heal themselves, but recovery is helped if they are kept still and in the right position. This means surrounding an injured arm or leg, for example, with a plaster cast to keep the bone still and protected from knocks, or putting pins or plates through or around the bone to hold it in place inside the body.

Traction

Sometimes muscles can tighten around injured bones. This puts strain on the break and causes the muscles to shorten. To prevent this, a patient's broken limb may be put into a special system of weights and pulleys called traction, in which the limb is supported but slightly stretched to relieve pressure on the injury.

Fractured humerus

The patient in the X-ray below has suffered a severe fracture of the upper arm bone, or humerus. Such a fracture would take six to eight weeks to heal.

Fractured thigh

A fractured thigh bone, or femur (below), is a common injury in older people suffering from brittle bones, or osteoporosis.

How a bone heals

When a bone breaks, blood from the damaged blood vessels in the bone marrow makes a clot around the fracture. New cartilage forms and holds the two parts of the bone together, making a natural splint. Bone cells gradually take over and new bone grows, knitting the break together.

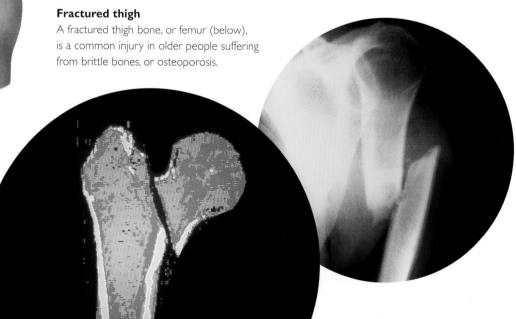

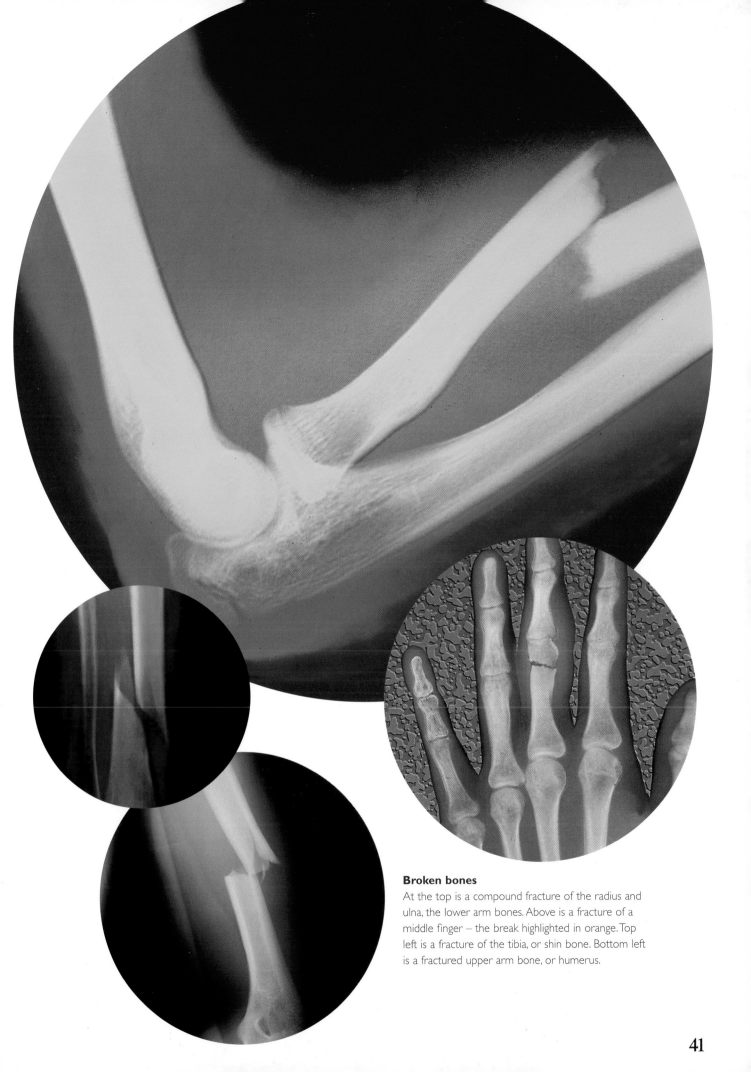

Broken bones

At the top is a compound fracture of the radius and ulna, the lower arm bones. Above is a fracture of a middle finger – the break highlighted in orange. Top left is a fracture of the tibia, or shin bone. Bottom left is a fractured upper arm bone, or humerus.

BONES & FOSSILS

Dinosaur giant
A palaeontologist examines the fossilized jaw bone and teeth of a giant meat-eating dinosaur discovered in Argentina in 1993. This dinosaur, named Gigantosaurus, was probably even larger than Tyrannosaurus, up until now thought to be the biggest ever land predator.

Much of what we know about life in the past comes from studying fossils of prehistoric animals and early humans.

Fossils are the remains of dead animals, which have lain embedded in rock and gradually turned to stone themselves. It is usually the harder parts of the body, such as bones and teeth, that are fossilized — soft parts of the body rot away.

Imagine a dinosaur dying millions of years ago. Once most of its flesh was eaten by other creatures, the rest would have gradually decayed until only the skeleton and teeth were left. Gradually the bones would have been covered with sand and mud until they were buried in the earth. Over the years, rock minerals replaced the minerals in the bone. Eventually the bone became a stony fossil in the same shape as the original. If at a later date that land is eroded or disturbed, those fossils may once again come to the surface.

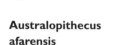

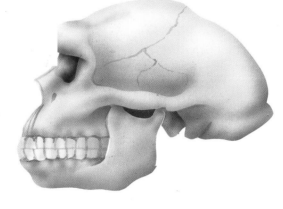

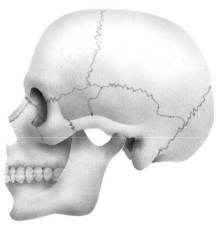

Australopithecus afarensis
This 'man-ape', an ancestor of our species, probably lived more than three million years ago. Skull fossils show that he had an apelike face and a much smaller brain than humans today.

Homo erectus
Known as 'upright man', this early human lived from more than a million years ago to about 100,000 years ago. His skull shows a flatter face and bigger brain case than Australopithecus.

Homo sapiens
This shows the skull of an early member of the modern human species, which developed about 100,000 years ago. The brain case is bigger than that of Homo erectus and there is no ridge across the brows.

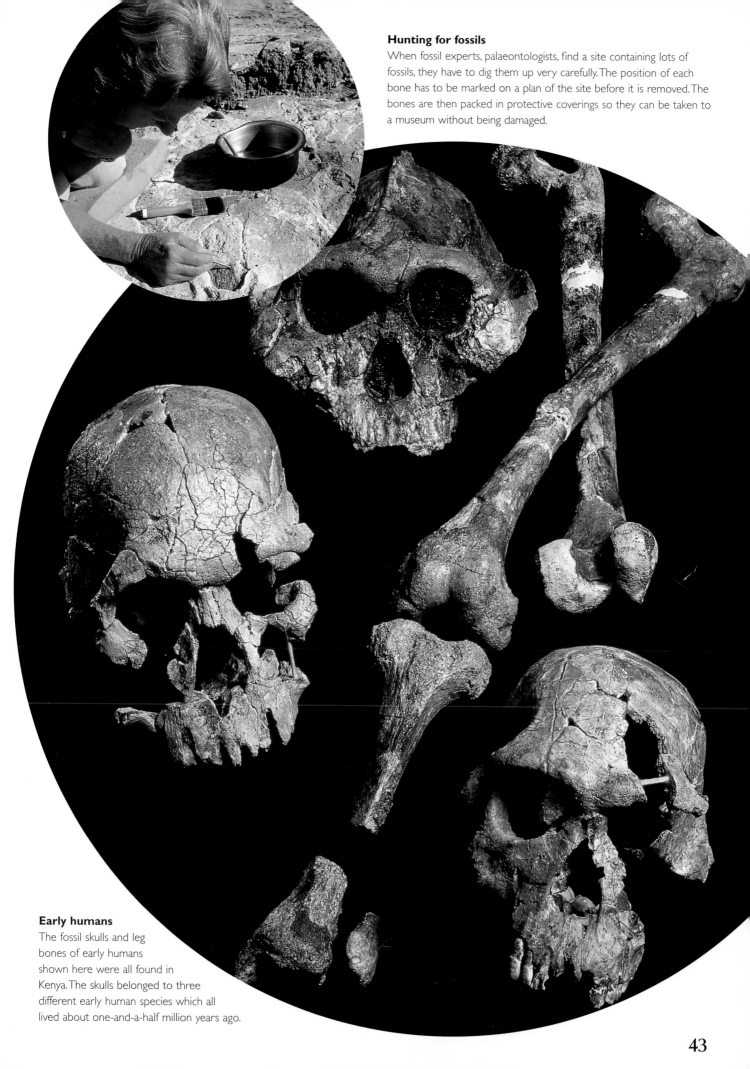

Hunting for fossils

When fossil experts, palaeontologists, find a site containing lots of fossils, they have to dig them up very carefully. The position of each bone has to be marked on a plan of the site before it is removed. The bones are then packed in protective coverings so they can be taken to a museum without being damaged.

Early humans

The fossil skulls and leg bones of early humans shown here were all found in Kenya. The skulls belonged to three different early human species which all lived about one-and-a-half million years ago.

BONE DISEASES

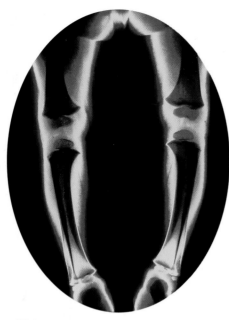

Bones are living parts of the body and need plenty of minerals and vitamins to keep them strong and healthy.

We get these minerals and vitamins by eating a healthy diet. Calcium and phosphorus are essential minerals for bone growth, and Vitamin D helps the bones to absorb these minerals. Vitamins A and C are also important for the development of bone and cartilage. Children who have a poor diet and lack vitamin D can suffer a disease called rickets. Their bones become soft and are easily deformed.

Bones store calcium for the rest of the body. If other parts lack calcium it may be taken from the bones, which can then become weak. Older people may suffer from lack of calcium. Their bones become thinner and they may suffer from a disease called osteoporosis, which causes the bones to become brittle and break easily. Research shows that adults actually need more calcium than growing children to keep their bones strong and healthy.

Rickets

The curving leg bones of this child are typical of the damage caused by rickets. The bones are so weak that they bend easily under stress.

Osteoarthritis

This disease mainly affects load-bearing joints such as the hips and knees, but can also occur in other parts of the body such as the hands and spine (below). The cartilage in the joints becomes worn away causing pain and loss of movement.

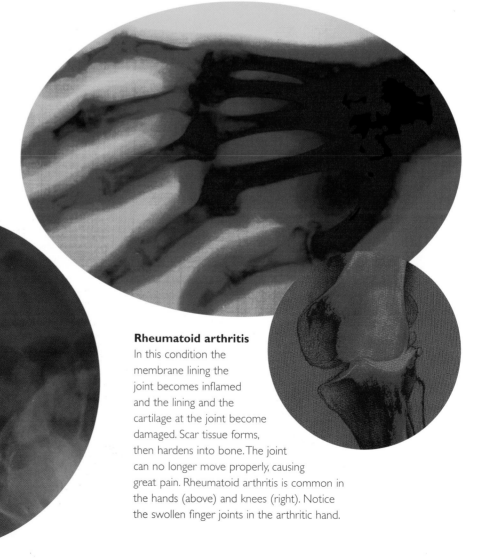

Rheumatoid arthritis

In this condition the membrane lining the joint becomes inflamed and the lining and the cartilage at the joint become damaged. Scar tissue forms, then hardens into bone. The joint can no longer move properly, causing great pain. Rheumatoid arthritis is common in the hands (above) and knees (right). Notice the swollen finger joints in the arthritic hand.

44

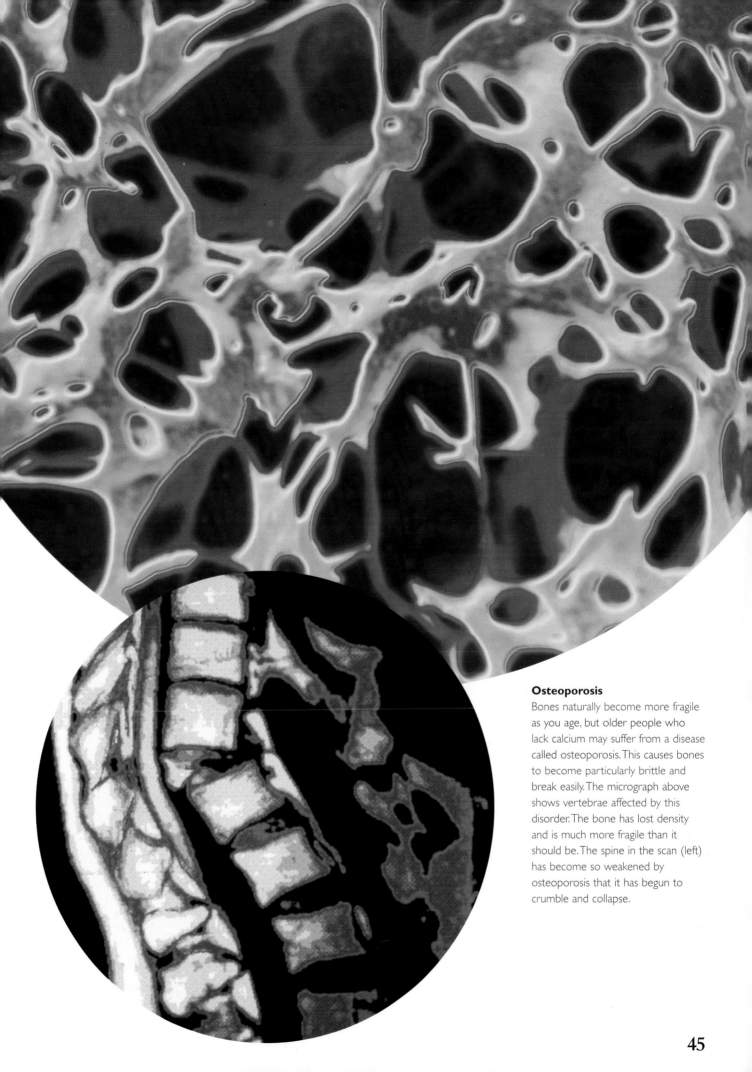

Osteoporosis

Bones naturally become more fragile as you age, but older people who lack calcium may suffer from a disease called osteoporosis. This causes bones to become particularly brittle and break easily. The micrograph above shows vertebrae affected by this disorder. The bone has lost density and is much more fragile than it should be. The spine in the scan (left) has become so weakened by osteoporosis that it has begun to crumble and collapse.

GLOSSARY

APPENDICULAR SKELETON
One of the two main divisions of the skeleton, this includes the bones of the shoulders, arms, hips and legs.

AXIAL SKELETON
One of the two main divisions of the skeleton, this includes the bones of the skull, spine and chest.

BONE MARROW
A soft substance inside bones. Red marrow, found in the cancellous parts of certain bones, makes red blood cells. Yellow marrow is a fatty substance.

CANCELLOUS BONE
One of the two types of bone, this has an open, honeycomb structure, which is light but strong.

CARPAL BONE
One of the eight small bones in the wrist. The carpal bones are arranged in two rows of four bones.

CARTILAGE
A tough bendy material that makes up the end of the nose and much of the external ears. It also covers the ends of bones where they meet at joints. The skeleton of a foetus is made entirely of cartilage, and gradually turns to bone.

CLAVICLE
Also known as the collar bone, this is a long slim bone at the base of the neck. It links the sternum and the scapula, or shoulder blade.

COMPACT BONE
One of the two types of bone, this is a dense substance made up of closely packed rods of bone called Haversian systems.

CRANIUM
The top of the skull, the cranium is made up of eight bones that protect the brain.

FEMUR
The long bone in the thigh and the longest bone in the human body.

FIBULA
One of the bones of the lower leg. The fibula is the smaller of the two bones.

FRACTURE
A break in a bone. A bone may be cracked, snapped through or shattered into many pieces, depending on the way it is damaged.

HUMERUS
The long bone in the upper part of the arm. It extends from the shoulder to the elbow.

JOINT
The point where two or more bones meet. Most joints, such as those at the hips, knees and elbows, allow movement. But fixed joints, such as those between the bones of the skull, are rigid, with no movement between them.

LIGAMENT
A thick band of fibrous tissue that links bones or cartilage and allows movement at joints.

OSTEOPOROSIS
A disease most common in older people lacking in calcium. The bones become thinner and more brittle and they break easily.

PATELLA
Also known as the kneecap, this is a small bone which is positioned over the knee joint.

PELVIS
A basin-shaped structure that helps support the top of the body. It is made up of the two hip bones - each of which consists of the ilium, ischium and pubis bones - and the sacrum and coccyx at the base of the spine.

PERIOSTEUM
A tough membrane covering the outside of bones. It contains lots of blood vessels and bone-making cells.

PHALANGES
These are the small separate bones in the fingers and toes.

RADIUS
One of the two lower arm bones. The radius is the shorter of the two and lies on the inside of the arm.

RIBS
One of twelve pairs of bones that curve round from the backbone to the chest. Together they form a bony cage that protects the heart and lungs.

SCAPULA
Also known as the shoulder blade, this is a flat, triangular-shaped bone in the shoulder. The upper arm is linked to the scapula by a ball and socket joint.

SPINE
The central support of the back of the body, the spine is made up of a series of small irregular-shaped bones called vertebrae.

STERNUM
Also called the breastbone, the sternum is a flat bone at the front of the chest to which most of the ribs are attached.

TARSAL BONES
One of the seven short bones in the ankle.

TENDON
A cord of fibrous tissue that attaches muscle to bone.

TIBIA
One of the two bones of the lower leg. The tibia is the larger of the two and is also known as the shinbone.

ULNA
One of the two bones of the lower arm. The ulna is the longer of the two and lies on the outside of the arm.

VERTEBRA
One of the small bones that make up the spine. It is made up of a round solid shape, called the body, attached to a bony tube through which the spinal cord passes. On the tube are bony fins to which muscles are attached.

INDEX

Acknowledgements

The publishers wish to thank the following for supplying photographs for this book: Robert Becker/Custom Medical Stock Photo/Science Photo Library (SPL) 7; BSIP DuCloux/SPL 41 (CL); John Bavosi/SPL 35 (BR); Biophoto Associates/SPL 44 (TL); Chris Bjornberg/SPL 41 (CR); BSIP, LECA/SPL 40 (CR); Scott Camazine/SPL 14 (T, B), 44 (C); Clinical Radiology Dept and Salisbury District Hospital/SPL 26 (BL), 28–9 (BL), 40 (BR), 41 (T); CNRI/SPL 25 (BR); CNRI/SPL 9 (TR); Dr Gilbert Faure/SPL 35 (BL); Gca-CNRI/SPL 24 (TL), 45 (B); GJLP-CNRI/SPL 18 (BC), 40 (BL); Carlos Goldin/SPL 42 (TL); James King-Holmes/SPL 20-1 (BR); Mehau Kulyk/SPL front cover (TC), 20–1 (TC), 24 (CL), 26 (BR); Matt Meadows/Peter Arnold Inc./SPL 41 (BL); Miles Kelly Archives 4 (TR), 15 (TL), 30 (CL, CR), 31 (TL, CL, C, CR), 34 (CR), 36 (BL, C), 37 (BL); Prof. P Motta/Dept of Anatomy/ University 'La Sapienza', Rome/SPL front cover (BR), 13 (TR), 33; Alfred Pasieka/SPL 45 (T); Princess Margaret Rose Orthopaedic Hospital/SPL 44 (BL, BR); John Reader/SPL 43 (TL, B); J C Revy/SPL 4 (BL), 12 (TL), 15 (CL); Dave Roberts/SPL 28–9 (TC); SPL 4 (CL), 6 (TL, CL, B), 23 (TR), 32 (TL); Secchi, Lecaque, Roussel, UCLAF, CNRI/SCL 3 (TL), 13 (BR); Pat Spillane 15 (TR, model Laura Saunter), 39 (TL, model Shoji Tanaka; BR, model Laura Saunter); James Stevenson/SPL 38 (BR); The Stock Market 24 (BR); Andrew Syred/SPL 12 (BL); Tony Stone Images 10 (L), 11 (TL, C, BR), 20–1 (BL), 28–9 (BC), 39 (CL).